Ultra Marathon Running

An Anthology on How Ultra Running
helps your mental health

Jason Pegler

chipmunkapublishing
the mental health publisher

Published by
Chipmunkapublishing
United Kingdom

http://www.chipmunkapublishing.com

Foreword.

I love running. I've managed to complete 10
Ironman triathlons but never ventured into Ultra
Running although I often daydream about it. I
reached out to some friends and groups on
Facebook and asked some ultra runners how
running helps their mental health. Runners all
have a reason why they run and how it helps
them. Ultra runners are inspirational people as
they keep running when others stop. They
overcome great mental and physical challenges
and keep going against all odds. Then they set
another goal and train for another race.

I hope this book inspires you to run or run more
and enjoy running as much as I do. Thanks so
much to the contributors. Big thanks to Dean
Karnazes one of the greatest Ultra Runners of all
time, and Samantha Mills who volunteered to do
some editing for us. Also thanks to each of you
who contributed to the book, Dean Karnazes,
Tracey Watson, Mike Pini, Alastair Bridgman,
Graeme Stewart, Paul Pickford, Sheila
Aavilesc, Oliver Smith, Nikki Yeo, Mario Frucci,
Louis Hylands, Liz McCarthy, Samantha
Mills, Jude Hancock, James Wright and Michael
Creighton.

Jason Pegler

Dean Karnazes

Give us an overview of how you got into running.
I blame it all on bad Tequila (laughter). I loved to run when I was younger, but gave it up when I hit my teens. Then, on the night of my 30th birthday, I found myself in a nightclub with some friends—doing what you do on your 30th birthday (i.e. drinking heavily)—when I felt this primordial urge to leave.

"*What?*" they questioned, "*It's only midnight; let's have another round of tequila.*"

Instead, I walked out of the nightclub and ran 30-miles to celebrate my 30th birthday. I ran straight through the night and it was the first time I'd run in over a decade. I was drunk and it almost killed me, but I kept going. That night forever changed the course of my life.

What is the most memorable moment you have had while running?
While I've had the great privilege of running and racing on all seven continents of earth, twice now, in some of the most extreme and exotic locations on the planet—from running a marathon to the South Pole to running across the Sahara Desert—my most memorable moment is running a 10K race with my daughter, Alexandria, on her 10th birthday. Nothing will ever surpass that moment.

What's your motivation? What gets you back out there running every day?
I love to run. I've never let that joy escape me. You don't need a lot of motivation to do what you love.

What has been your biggest challenge/barrier to success over the years and how did you overcome it to get to where you are today?
Me. I've been my biggest barrier. That's always the case. We let our perceived limitations restrict our potential. If we can just move out of the way of ourselves we're capable of some truly extraordinary things.

What's your approach and thoughts around the pain and suffering that's associated with ultra running? How important is it for you personally to push beyond comfort zones?
Comfort is overrated. We're so comfortable we're miserable. To me, pain and suffering are the essence of a life well lived. Never do I feel more alive than when struggling to overcome great pain and to persevere. Ultra running is the perfect medium to experience these emotions and test the limits of what is possible.

What advice would you give to your younger self, given the chance?
Buy Apple stock at six bucks a share (more laughter). Seriously, that would have changed things. But honestly, I don't think I'd be doing anything different. I'd just give it all to charity.

What lessons have you learned along the way and how do the basic principles of running translate to everyday life?

Success is achieved through baby steps. It's the little things you do each and every day, the extra five percent of effort you give to every task, that leads to greatness. Much of it is the quiet grunt work done behind the scenes, the paying your dues and doing what is necessary to perfect your craft. Nothing of greatness is ever achieved through shortcuts or by taking the path of least resistance. It all comes down to hard work.

How has running changed you as a person? Running has made me more humble. Running has taught me that the greatest joys in life are achieved through simplicity. The true measure of a man is what he can do without. As a runner, I don't need much. Just a pair of shoes and an open road.

What's next? What are you training for at the moment and what plans have you got in the pipeline?
I once ran 50 marathons, in all of the 50 US states, in 50 consecutive days. People said it would be impossible, but I somehow managed to pull it off. In fact, I enjoyed the experience so much I set my next BHAG (Big, Hairy, Audacious Goal) as running a marathon in every country of the world in a one-year timeline. There are currently 203 countries on the planet and I am working with the UN and the US State Department to get all of the necessary permits, passports and visas required to visit each and every one to run a marathon. That is my dream.

Tracey Watson

When you first started running:

I was a keen runner at school and one of the few girls in my year that loved cross-country. I was small, slim and ran like a whippet. When I reached my teens, boys and alcohol got in the way. I realised something had to change, when at the age of 35, I climbed a flight of stairs at work and was seriously out of breath. It was a reality check, I was three stone overweight, did no exercise, liked junk food and always worked late. I started Tae Kwon Do (TKD) to get fit and relieve stress but didn't appreciate that you had to kick and punch people (despite it being a martial art) and I was terrified of sparring to start with. I quickly began to enjoy TKD though and realised that I had to get fitter to improve at it. I joined a gym and slowly started running. It was a walk-run affair to start with and eventually I could manage 4 slow miles on the treadmill. I met someone at the gym who persuaded me to run outdoors. My first run was terrifying – I panicked because I couldn't breathe, but the lady I was running with persisted. She said she would let me slow down, but I couldn't stop and before I knew it I had run 5 miles. I began running regularly and my distances slowly increased.

What is the furthest distance you have run, how long did it take and where?

Please include the name and location of the race. Your preparation how the race went and how you felt afterwards

I had no idea what I was doing when I lined up at the start of a trail half marathon. It was my first race and I was terrified. It didn't help that the weather was terrible and the course was muddy and hilly. I was delighted to finish but struggled to walk down the stairs for a few days afterwards. A few more years and half marathons later, I was drawn by the lure of the marathon (like a lot of runners). I really got into trail running, when I did the 3 Forts Challenge – 27.2 miles and 3,500ft of ascent on the South Downs Way. The views, peace and solitude were definitely my thing. I ran more marathons and did my first 50km distance, which didn't seem too bad. I knew by then I preferred the trail to the road. A year later and the night before the Brighton marathon, I saw on social media that a friend had completed the South Downs Way 50 (50 miles from Worthing to Eastbourne). We were similar-paced runners and I started to wonder if I might be able to do something like it too. It would be running in a place that I loved, after all. I signed up that summer and began training. It was the toughest thing I had ever done, I was so unprepared as this was an ultra with cut-offs and serious hills, I was running with a backpack, carrying kit, having to navigate. I had no idea what to do – I just kept topping up on food, salt tablets and fluid. I hadn't even figured I was going to have to run on my own in the dark. When I reached the final trig point and saw the lights of Eastbourne glowing orange below, I knew that against all odds I had done it. The sense of achievement was incredible when I reached the finish. My journey led me to complete the North Downs Way 50 a few weeks later when a last minute place became available, then I jumped right in and booked a place on the Autumn 100. It's four out-and-back runs of 25 miles from Goring in Oxfordshire. Again, I was probably still underprepared and didn't know what to expect. I was running around 35-50 miles a week at that stage. I did a recce of the entire route, trained with my kit more thoroughly and finished it in 26 hours, 50 minutes. It's a journey that led me to run another 12 100-mile races amongst others.

How often you run:
I run 6-7 days a week, sometimes twice a day. There are days when I have to squeeze it in – a quick 4 miles before work, another session with a running club in the evening. It's a habit, like brushing your teeth really. I run anywhere between 50-70 miles a week and fit in strength and conditioning and spin classes too. My kit is always packed and ready to go. I suppose it's just become part of my life and even when I don't feel like doing it, I always feel better when it's done.

What you enjoy about running:
The peace and solitude. Being fortunate enough to run in some beautiful places and see some incredible things. The older I get, the less I am bothered about times or achievement. If I get a PB, it's a bonus, the icing on the cake, but I don't

chase it. I have met some amazing people too – there's a saying that misery loves company and that's definitely true of this sport. One of the joys about ultras is the sense that everyone wants to help each other, people just want others to finish. It's the only time I have ever had people wait for me to catch up so they can hold a gate open for me. Whenever I lose faith in human nature, ultra running reminds me of all that is good in the world.

How running helps your mental health:
Running is like meditation – it's just the sound of my feet and my breathing. It clears my head, balances my mood, puts life's problems in perspective. It's been a comfort-blanket in difficult times, a way to cope with bereavement and stress. There's nothing like a morning run watching the sunrise to put a smile on your face. It's the sheer joy of running through a field of bright green barley or golden corn. I love the way it brings you in touch with the seasons, it's like you chase the year. The months are marked by the colours, the changes in the landscape and smells. The exhilaration of running in the rain, the crunch of pine cones underfoot, the woods that seem like they are on fire on a sunny autumn day. The pleasure of being wet, cold and muddy and warming up. There is nothing like the satisfaction of climbing a hill and seeing the views stretch for miles in front of you, a ribbon of chalk path behind and ahead. Yes, you are on top of the world. Running through the night with a full moon, head torches bobbing in the hills, seeing the lights of ships in the sea, cars and streetlights below.

Why you enjoy running:
The balance it brings to life, the connection with
nature and seasons. The incredible stuff I get to
see. The list goes on really. The amazing sense of
achievement when you deal with what scares you
– like running through the woods and fields on
your own, in the dark. Then there's crossing the
line after 100 miles of running for hours and hours.
Only you know what it took for you to get there,
what you have endured; how hard you pushed.
Every time I stand on the start line of an ultra, I
know it's not a given I will finish and I never take it
for granted. It's best to stay humble, for the day
will come when I can no longer do this stuff, but I
want to look back and know I enjoyed it and be
thankful for what it brought to my life.

What running teaches you about life?
It's taught me so much, but mostly that I am braver
than I believe, stronger than I seem and smarter
than I think. I am so much more confident in life
generally. I have learnt to break things down into
small bite-size chunks to get it done. I push myself
to get things done if I don't want to, focusing on
the benefits at the end. All the times I have been
terrified of giving presentations at work or I have to
do something uncomfortable, I remind myself that
I can run 100 miles, on my own and in the dark. I
can deal with problems when they arise, thinking
on my feet. Funnily enough, running has taught
me who my true friends are too and now I spend
my time and associate myself with those that

share my views and how I see the world. I don't care what others think. For a little while I got caught up in the whole thing of feeling I had to go faster, I had to run further. I have returned to what I truly want to do and the joy for me is all about the journey. I now have the confidence to do what I want – what makes me happy!

Any future running goals?
Where do I start? My ultimate race would be the Northburn 100 in New Zealand or Two Oceans in South Africa. I used to think I wanted to go further than 100 miles, but actually it's no longer about the distance, it's the journey and the people. I had a crack at the Spine Race but got injured during the first day. It was my own fault for being a numpty, but again, a valuable life lesson. At the time I was upset as it was my first DNF, but in a strange way I am grateful for the experience, I learned a lot, I am proud of my ability to care for myself when badly injured and alone on the moors on a freezing cold January night. If I pluck up the courage again, I may return to the Spine, but probably the shorter distance Challenger first and I want to get more mountain running experience.

Anything you want to include about your job, family, where you live, where you are from and future life situation and goals?
I'm average, not particularly fast, but proof that if you want something and work hard enough, you'll succeed. I juggle a busy job in marketing with training to do some tough distances. I'm hugely lucky to have a great husband who crews me and

is stupidly proud of me, always believes in me, but also knows when to swear at me, tell me to toughen up and get it done. My family are pretty amazing too – although my little sister has only just forgiven me for pacing duties on the North Downs 100 and the hundreds of steps at Detling. My mum is my number one fan and always makes me smile – she told me that I smelt horrible, I should be running not walking and asked if I wanted a pot noodle at 85 miles into a race.

Any other ultras you have loved doing or found the toughest, and times?
I often return to Centurion events and sometimes get teased about it, but do you know what, 100 miles is blooming hard, so you might as well pick a race you love. My favourite is the South Downs Way 100, the route is beautiful, it feels like an old friend; especially the last 50 miles (I guess I have a soft spot as it was my first serious ultra). This year has been pretty tough and I joke that it's involved more vomit than I care to remember. I am not good in the heat and suffered on the Thames Path 100, throwing up at 24 miles outside one of the most expensive properties on the river. The South Downs 100 was humid but a bit more bearable, then it warmed up nicely again for the North Downs 100. I managed the heat a little better and ran 50 miles with ice in my cap, bra and buff to keep my temperature and heart rate down, but it was probably the most uncomfortable race I have done. My last race in this year's 100-mile slam was another favourite, the Autumn 100. It was unseasonably warm for that time of year and I

spent a fair bit of time being sick from 24 to 38 miles (run, puke, run), but I hung tough, forced the food, salt and water in to bring myself back to life in the second half of the race (see – never give up). The heavens opened at 4am in the morning and I ran 7 hours in torrential rain to get my grand slam buckle. Not my fastest, but certainly my proudest year of running and even better to cross the line with family and friends waiting.

Mike Pini

I found my love of running at secondary school where I surprised the sports teachers by setting a new 1500m record and, inspired by the brilliant British trio of Steve Ovett, Seb Coe and Steve Cram, won a couple of school district championships. For a while I tried to erase the memory of my failed attempt at a hat-trick of district golds (for some reason I dipped for the finish line 10m early and ended up third) but have long since realised that this unfortunate event taught me how to cope with 'failure' – but what's failure in running anyway? Every run is a success, right?

After completing ten or so marathons I thought I'd built up enough stamina to enter an ultra marathon (an ultra marathon is any distance longer than a marathon, but typically starts at around 31 miles/50km). And after completing a few ultra marathons, up to 42 miles, I decided to attempt a 62 mile/100km race. Rather than pay a huge wad of cash to take part in a big commercial event, I saw the more affordable, low-key Ham & Lyme race advertised by the very friendly Albion Running. It was David Unwin's first event as a Race Director and he began his pre-race briefing, at Ham Hill Country Park in Somerset, with "Please don't die!" Back in July 2015 the route largely followed the Liberty Trail across the county border into Lyme Regis on Dorset's Jurassic Coast and all the way back again. However, many runners failed to bring the maps provided or a compass so I found myself navigating for five or six others most of the way to the town made famous for its dinosaur fossils.

Then, on the way back north, me and another lad I was running with, Steve, caught up with the two 100km race leaders. The race turned a little surreal at this point. We'd all taken wrong turns at various points and were shattered so we agreed to run only on the flat and downhill stretches, but walk the inclines together. My longest race to date was 42 miles so I felt a little inexperienced compared to my three fellow competitors who had all run races of at least 100 miles. Too fatigued to fight it out for first place, Steve and I decided to let the other two go ahead. But then disaster struck and we got seriously lost… At one stage we had to ask three guys sitting on the grass in a park for help.

"To Lyme Regis and back? Just get a car, man," they replied, puffing out clouds of smoke, before pointing us in the right direction. Later, after the final aid station, we took another wrong turn. And then it got dark. Eventually, at around 10:30pm, we crossed the finish line together in joint fifth place with other runners whom the Race Director's brother had rescued from the course.

Would I do that race again? Of course I would, especially as it starts the other way around next year, from Lyme Regis, and as any runner knows, a slight change to the route gives us a little extra incentive to have another go at it.

Apart from the obvious mistakes of veering off course, I made two other errors that day, which can lose one a lot of time on long runs: the first was to eat too much at the first and second aid stations. Moving on a half-full belly isn't much fun; and I hadn't drunk enough fluids, but this didn't occur to me until I finished when I thought to myself, 'I haven't peed in 14 hours'. I was dehydrated, slightly disappointed with my time, but also pleased to have completed the 100km course (I probably covered 105km in all).

The next day I ate for England – it was a good plan to arrange a barbecue for friends – but I could barely move my legs to reach for another plate of food.

Preparation for this race was simple. While the internet is full of training plans for any target time for 5km to the marathon, running 50 miles or more seems to be simply about getting as much time on the feet as possible. My approach was to run 10 or 12 miles the day after a hard marathon race and then run again the next day.

It's important to train when the legs are tired, gradually increase weekly mileage and listen to the body. I generally try to run a consistent volume of miles every week and then ramp it up when training for a race. I prefer to run on five or six days of the week and then take extra rest days when I feel that I need them.

It takes experience to get this balance right, though, and experience only comes by getting outside and running, running with others, talking to coaches and entering races.

Despite the distance, that 100km wasn't my toughest race, possibly because my average pace was actually relatively slow. My toughest single-day event was probably the Ultimate Trails 55km in the Lake District two years later, on 1 July, 2017. The terrain was rugged, the hills were brutal and the wind was wicked in the afternoon. I remember swearing loudly at the wind when I felt particularly tired, before realising a volunteer marshal was standing just up the road. "F£$% off, wind!... Oh, thanks Marshal. This way? Thanks."

The 36 miles took me almost 7 hours. Before we started, I thought, 'how hard can 10 minute-miles be?' Very hard. I had to walk quite a bit in places. It was my lowest-placed finish in an ultra marathon race, but I was really pleased, and I was back at race HQ in time to recover, shower and head to the pub with some fellow athletes.

One of the many great things about running is that it can make you feel really good while doing it, then make you feel extremely tired and sometimes quite emotional, and then, once you've completed the challenge, it can make you feel elated for a long time.

Covering long distances under your own steam is a simple but powerful pleasure that can be achieved almost anywhere in almost any weather. It's no wonder that people get 'marathon jealousy'.

A year later I entered my first multi-day race. Saltmarsh 75 was a flat, 75-mile course round the beautiful Essex coastline. I grew up in the county, my parents still lived nearby, I wanted to test myself over two days, and my maternal grandmother's maiden name was Saltmarsh. Tick, tick, tick, tick.

Training consisted of running back-to-back long runs and increasing the distance as I got nearer to the day so that I could mimic the event conditions as best I could. However, I got distracted by a chance to run one of my favourite local marathons a month before and the tapering for, and recovery from that, might have affected my Saltmarsh preparation a little.

The two-day race, held in early October 2018, was very challenging simply because of the short recovery time from finishing day one at 2:45pm-ish to resuming the race at 8am the next day. Moving off the start line on the Sunday revealed my right knee to be quite stiff and for a mile or so I wondered how on earth I was going to reach the finish line 37 miles farther round the coast. What doesn't kill you…

It's fair to say I'm possibly completely hooked on running. The more I run the more I feel like running. Whereas ten years ago I would easily put off going out the door if it was raining and there was something good to watch on TV, these days the 'barrier' to going out is tiny; I'm almost on autopilot tying my laces and heading out into the wind or rain; I'm compelled to run.

I think anyone would feel like this if they ran several times a week for a sustained period of time. The endorphins, dopamine and serotonin rise and rise and increase motivation. Of course I lose my mojo from time to time, but it doesn't last long – a few days, perhaps.

Running is immensely enjoyable in many different ways. But I believe that not everyone feels this deep passion unless they run a lot. The feelings I get now I regularly run between 40 to 60 miles per week are certainly different than those I remember when I ran 5 or 10. But I'll be honest; running more than 60 miles per week can feel more like a part-time job and sometimes like a chore. This is especially true when doing double-training days, which I did a lot while preparing for a marathon Personal Best (PB) attempt. It's not easy getting five or six easy miles under the feet in the morning, going to work and then doing 45 minutes of intervals in the evening. The running is mostly still fun, but I found stretching and showering twice a day quite tedious. It makes you wonder how professional athletes stay highly motivated over extended periods of time.

There's a definite sense of freedom, especially on trails in the open countryside or on quiet country lanes, and this is more intensive when alone.

Running with someone else or in groups is great for chatting to like-minded people and discovering where they like to run. The goals one can set oneself in running are only limited by one's imagination – I like running by feeling, but numbers can be used in a multitude of ways to motivate and inspire.

Attempting PBs, running the furthest distance ever, on x number of consecutive days, getting y number of miles in each month, having a yearly target, attending as many parkrun venues or completing the parkrun alphabet, marathons in different counties, in different climates and biomes… the list gets longer…

It's also the simplicity. A pair of running trainers is all you need. Yes, a good vest or t-shirt and decent shorts and appropriate socks make a big difference, but, like with all sports and outdoor pursuits, the correct footwear is essential to enhance enjoyment and performance.

Lessons can be learnt from any sport but I've found that endurance running has helped me to be calmer and more patient, dedicated and disciplined. I feel more honest with myself when I've run, feel like I've done something worthwhile, feel like I've not been lazy that day.

I reckon I'd need a whole book to list my running goals, and I need to live to at least 300 years old, and still be in good shape, to achieve them all.

Having something to look forward to achieving, as well as getting physical and mental exercise, is one of the keys to a long life in my view.

I'd like to complete 100 marathons, although I'm in no rush and I try to perform my best in every one. And then, how many ultra marathons?

My brother has challenged me to run a marathon in every county in England, which I'm slowly getting through, but where next, the counties of Wales and Scotland? Marathons in every country in Europe? The world? Britain's national trails, perhaps. I'd like to run/walk them all, but have many yet to do.

There are now well over 500 parkrun venues (some people are trying to complete them all) in the UK and you'll find them in more than 15 countries around the globe.

And now I've joined the coaching team at my club, Hook Runners, I'm trying to help others achieve their goals, too. Quite a few members are keen to run their first marathons or improve their PBs, so it would be rewarding to help them, in a small way. It's a surprisingly wonderful feeling running with someone when they complete their furthest distance without stopping.

Whenever I extend my own distance PB it's like a journey into the unknown, learning more about myself, literally breaking new ground. Time and pace go out of the window – it's just about getting each mile under the feet and slowly making it to the target mileage, and then trying to go a bit further.

You never know who or what you might see when you go for a run. Especially in unusual places. I was lucky enough to travel through 10 countries in Latin America in 2015/16 and during this time spent four weeks in Bolivia. I didn't see a single other runner and the locals, who mostly wore traditional clothes, looked at me, in my shorts and T-shirt, like I was from Mars.

Perhaps it was the altitude. I couldn't resist experiencing struggling up and down hills at 3,700m / 2.3 miles above sea level. At this height oxygen concentration in the air is around only 60% of what it is on a beach at sea level, so it felt like one of my lungs had been removed.

One Saturday afternoon I trotted out along the shore of Lake Titicaca. I intended an out-and-back run, 2.5 miles each way. Heading round a steep bend perhaps 400m before this point, a large group of men and boys were standing around a few cars. They turned to me and all instantly burst out laughing. I said, "*hola, hola*" and smiled back, moving on. Minutes later I had to turn around to retrace my steps. This time the wives, sisters, mums, girlfriends and daughters all stood together waiting for me. They roared with laughter and were still laughing as I ran the bend. But this time, to my surprise, the men and boys stood and all clapped and cheered loudly for me. "*Gracias*, *muchas gracias*," I said, with a huge smile on my face. It was the most heart-warming moment I experienced in the Andean country. It's moments like these that are worth running in unusual places for – even with just the equivalent of one lung working.

Three days later I ran on Isla del Sol, a picturesque Bolivian island in the middle of Lake Titicaca. A man was walking in the same direction and called to me as I overtook him. "*Amigo!*" I stopped and said hello and he started gesturing, wanting to exchange my GPS watch with his small bedside alarm clock. "*Calendario, calendario*," he said, pointing at his possession. My limited Spanish language skills didn't allow me to explain that my device could measure my movements, measure my pace, or that all my data for Latin America was stored on it, or that the battery would die in two hours without the charger. Needless to say, we didn't swap.

And it's amazing how exciting running in iconic places can be, too, how much happiness it can bring. Months earlier, on my first full day in Brazil I just had to run along the famous Copacabana and Ipanema beaches – just to say I'd done it, but more importantly to experience it.

A few months later, after Bolivia, and minutes after surviving a hair-raising, cliff-edge road journey, I ran 10km beside a railway track to the base of the hills upon which Machu Picchu sits. It was the perfect way to save cash from the pricey train fare (my girlfriend kindly lugged two backpacks onto the train). Other backpackers chose to walk the route but the look on their faces when they saw me running; it was a picture. The next day I walked/ran up to the famous Inca site and then onwards and upwards to see the amazing views of the whole, magnificent setting.

So why not run in iconic places, or places special to you? You don't need to pay for organised events to get the enormous satisfaction and reward that putting one step in front of the other and repeating it can bring you.

Run in the place you were born, run up your favourite hill, run on Christmas Day dressed as Santa, run dressed as a gorilla. I did this once, in September 2004 in aid of the Great Gorilla Foundation. I was scanning events on a well-known running website when my friend looked over my shoulder. "There, that's the one for you! I'll sponsor you, here's a tenner." I entered on the spot and a month or two later was plodding the streets of London with six hundred other fundraisers, all in full gorilla costume. The clever organisers encouraged us to wear fancy dress over the gorilla suits. I'd left it a bit late so my girlfriend's dad lent me a plastic Viking helmet, a long blonde wig and large, plastic boobs. When we gathered near the start line, a young lad, possibly about nine or ten years old, holding his mum's hand, said something to her. They weren't in costume but were obviously there to support someone else. I heard her reply, "You want to say hello to that one? Ok." And she brought him over to meet me. Disguised as a Viking gorilla-warrior princess I tried not to laugh at the lad's wishes and wondered what his mum was thinking of them.

Lots of people on the capital's streets took photos of us all and some came up to get a closer look. An Asian bloke, possibly a tourist, just couldn't stop staring at my plastic breasts. So I slowed to a walk, made myself bigger and strode over to him. He froze, wide-eyed. "Where have you been all my life?" I said in a loud, gruff voice and gave him a big hug. He was stiff as a board from head to toe. Two tradesmen stepped out of a building they were working in, looked at me and one remarked, "They're bigger than my wife's." Two minutes later four German girls, all tourists together in the city, demanded photos with me, one by one. My brother met me metres from the finish to get in the pics. It was the most fun four miles I've ever run.

Even a standard road race can be fun. Seeing people line the streets to cheer everybody on is incredibly uplifting. Adults clapping and shouting encouragement, and children cheering, offering sweets and attempting high five or low fives is all incredibly uplifting. I once had six or seven kids in a row try to do this. It was a mini roller-coaster of low and high fives, but I somehow 'fived' them all, without breaking my stride, and heard an accompanying adult remark, "Wow, that was excellent." It's all part of the fun of running.

Alastair Bridgman

It's 17th November 2018, 1am in the morning and I'm standing in a small village in Northern Lanzarote, waiting for a bus to take me to a start line. I am about to start the Haria Extreme, a 100km ultra-marathon. How on earth did I get here?

To answer that question, I have to go back to late 2011. I'm 39 years old and conscious that I will be turning 40 next year. The Olympics are about to come to London and enthusiasm around the country is building for the event.

I was sporty as a child and teenager, but during adulthood and especially in the last 10 years, I have not really had any consistent form of exercise. So, I decide to go for a run. It didn't last long, I barely made it out of my estate before I had to stop. In going home, I knew I wasn't happy being this unfit so decided to take up running.

It took a few months to get to a point where I could run consistently without stopping for a few miles, but I just gradually built on each run, starting twice a week and moving on to three times a week. At the time my marriage was going through a difficult period and I quickly found that running gave me a better sense of perspective and allowed me to deal with my thoughts, worries and concerns in a rational manner. Running quickly became a companion and friend.

My original goal was to be able to run 10 miles at the weekend, with a couple of shorter runs in the week to keep my fitness up. As I progressed to this goal I became aware the half marathon distance was only a few miles more, so I altered my goal. Then five months after that first run I completed my first half marathon. Although before the race I had only got to 9 miles as my longest run, I was surprised I managed to keep going and quickly realised that I was able to do more.

With Bradley Wiggins winning the Tour de France in 2012, just before the Olympics, there was a real surge in cycling popularity. This looked very cool and the thought of gradually moving up those mountains became a real incentive. I joined a triathlon six-week start-up programme and did my first sprint triathlon six weeks later.

I had caught the bug, and trained in swimming, cycling and running now. So much so, that 12 months later I was standing on a beach in Lanzarote in my first Ironman. By this point I was really enjoying endurance events, pushing myself to see what I could achieve, whilst dealing with my thoughts and my mind persuading me to stop. It really appealed to me that in my 40's I was showing myself I could do things I had never done before. They say when you are under pressure you find out who you really are, and I was finding that I wouldn't quit and would just keep going. I liked that about myself. I also found that it was helping in life and work, being able to see through the people who were not being honest and removing people from your life who didn't support or value you.

At the time my marriage wasn't getting better. I would eventually get separated in 2016 and divorced in 2017 and I know a lot of people assume that exercise led to this, but the truth is the reason for the marriage being over had happened before I ever went for that first run. Looking back, running was initially filling a hole that was created by these difficulties and this enabled me to keep a perspective on problems and issues, without thoughts running away in my head and catastrophising events. So rather than be the reason for the breakdown, I now know it gave me the strength to work through it. Through the next few years, between 2013 and 2017, I did a mix of long-distance triathlons, including 12 half Ironmans and five Ironmans. I also took on ultra-marathons including a couple of 50-milers, a 50km, two and three-day ultras and the Marathon des Sables.

Then in 2017 when training for my fifth Ironman I just wasn't motivated anymore for triathlons. The cycling and swimming seemed like chores rather than something to enjoy, so after Ironman South Africa in 2017, I solely concentrated on running. In the early days I was amazed how inclusive running was. People would chat with you and be generally interested in what you had to say. Other runners were supportive when you needed help and pleased for you when you did well. There wasn't a sign of over-competitiveness or others bringing you down to make themselves better. I found the culture in running was that we were all on our own journeys and happy to meet others traveling along a similar path. It is something that has kept me in running and I have also tried to encourage others into the sport for these reasons to show the inclusive nature of the sport.

During this time, I also met my new partner through a local running club. A new community running club was set up in late 2016 in my village and in early 2017 I met a wonderful lady who had been going through a similar period in her life but had used parkrun to help her. We first spoke on a Sunday long run and I immediately found her easy to talk to. Over the next month we became friends and then about four weeks later decided to start dating.

After the Ironman, I decided I wanted to concentrate on the marathon and get back to enjoying myself and being part of a more inclusive sport. It did take a while for my legs to get used to the run-only exercise plan. I enjoyed running with my new partner and we entered events together and had weekends away based around events, which we have also shared with friends. I found my running started getting quicker as a result and consistently started finding myself at the top end of races, often picking up overall top three or age group winner awards.

But back to Lanzarote. The island has always fascinated me. Having done the Ironman there twice, the part I enjoyed most was the bike ride through the mountains in the northern part of the island. I was really drawn to this and when I saw there was an ultra event in November decided to enter. I wanted to share this with my new partner and her children, so we made a week-long holiday out of it to explore the region and really find out what this part of the island is about. We stayed in Haria for the week, with the race coming in the middle of the holiday.

Leading up to the event I had been suffering from niggling pains but continued to train. I did get away with a few warm-up races including a marathon but didn't manage to shake off the niggles.

On the bus trip down to the start line my hamstrings were tight and hurting sitting on the bus. I realised this wasn't pre-race concerns, but was going to be a case of completing rather than competing. In truth if this was in the UK I would have pulled out, but as I was abroad and brought loved ones with me, the decision to pull out was a lot harder to make. This wasn't bothering me too much, I had had a successful season with plenty of PBs and podium finishes, and this was all about seeing the island and experiencing the mountains and volcanic region.

It was dark when we got to the start line and after about an hour of hanging around we got going.

Four miles into the race my legs were hurting more, and I quickly decided to try and conserve my legs by walking the up and down hill sections. This reinforced my concerns that it was going to be a long day out. This run/walk continued with the walking parts becoming more frequent, but by the halfway point, walking was becoming painful and slow.

The first time I met with my partner and her children was at mile 31, where she immediately saw I was in trouble. I could see the concern on her face despite me trying to reassure her, and I carried on. Walking was about the only thing I could do now and that was becoming painful. The second half of the race had three climbs and over 2,500ft of climbing on each of them, with two of them being technical as well.

It was becoming a painful, slow slog and as I mentioned earlier I have found I do not quit. I have realised that in life what can be your greatest strength can also be your greatest weakness. I was going beyond the point of toughing it out and now was just creating injury problems for myself. At the lunch stop in Arrieta, I changed shoes, had some food and was feeling a bit more revitalised. The concern on my partner's face was worrying me and I did hear her say to someone "I don't know what to do" which hit my heart in a big way.

Next was the climb up to Mirador. During the climb bad weather set in and by the time we got to the top of the mountain we were in a cloud. By this time the rain was coming at us horizontally and I was having trouble just staying upright in the gale-force winds. By the time I got to the top of Mirador, and despite wearing my rain jacket, fleece and underlayer I was cold and shaking uncontrollably. I thought I may get some respite at the aid station, but the aid station had largely blown away, although to their credit some very enthusiastic kids were still filling water bottles. I was a little bemused by this and the fact that they were not holding people here until the weather cleared up. People were leaving the aid station, disorientated by the weather, in the wrong direction and there was just general confusion amongst everyone.

I set off from Mirador and found myself unable to control my emotions. With seeing my partner extremely concerned and tearful, the weather and my general condition I found myself crying uncontrollably. It's not the first time this has happened, this has happened a few times previously in other events lasting 10-plus hours towards the end. I have found there is no real reason for doing this. It is just a reaction to pushing your body and mind to an extreme limit. I cannot make sense of my emotions, the ability to calculate how far I have to go has long disappeared and I have lost the emotional strength to comprehend what is happening. About a mile from the aid station I found a fellow Englishman at the side of the road asking if I spoke English. I said I did, then he asked if I spoke Spanish. I didn't. It turned out he had cramp and tried phoning the SOS number only to find they didn't speak English. As we were planning what to do next a van came down the road and we both immediately assumed that was for him, he thanked me, and I continued to struggle on. It was only when the van pulled up to me that I realised that something else was up. It turns out they had stopped the race due to the bad weather. In returning back to Mirador I found my friend still on the side of the road wondering what had just happened.

He said they had told him he's finished. He said yes, he was finished, so he went to get in the back, and they drove off without him, much to his confusion. I explained the race was over, and we made our way back to the top, where luckily my partner was still parked and she drove us back. It was over, 85km completed, approximately 15km to go and the weather had caused the event to stop.

Since coming home I have had a lot of comments suggesting it was a shame that the event was stopped and commiserations for me. I don't see it this way. I went to explore northern Lanzarote. I achieved that. I understand and appreciate where these comments come from and on the surface it was a DNF, injury and a much slower than normal pace, but I am ok with all of this.

In some regards I see this as my biggest achievement. Despite coming first in several races, I have never had to battle for as long as I did on the 17th November and in so much pain. I am proud of myself for not giving up, only to be stopped eventually by the weather. Having travelled 50 miles in pain I can hold my head up high.

Running has played a big part in my life. It has helped me through the bad times and made sense of issues in my life and allowed me to move forwards. I will always say running is an honest companion. It will not give you anything you do not work for. It does not allow you to hide behind team-mates or rely on others. But if you respect it, it can give you so much, both in sporting rewards and in life.

Running on the surface has allowed me to meet some very special and honest people with shared goals. Rarely do I find someone who wouldn't help another in need and this is something the sport should be most proud of. It has allowed me to see parts of the UK and the world I otherwise wouldn't have access to, and to accomplish things I thought I never would. As well as running experiences, it has allowed me to grow as an individual. I have found that I am far more resilient than I ever thought, and running has allowed me to deal with life issues with a better perspective. It has allowed me to see those who aren't supportive to you and prefer to put you down. I have realised I don't need to hang on and can surround myself with more positive friends and colleges.

I have also met my partner through running and we will be getting married in 2019, so it has given me a new life. Without running and these personal qualities that have allowed me to grow, I wouldn't be in such a good place today. So I have a lot to thank running for, and a lot to look forward to in the future.

Graeme Stewart

My story begins at sea... off the island of Maui, in the Pacific, in about fifteen metres of seawater, in 1997.

I was on honeymoon, doing a course to learn about rebreathers for domestic diving, which is a piece of equipment that uses a closed loop to re-oxygenate your exhaled breath. Except mine had a blockage impeding the oxygen getting into the loop, so all I was breathing was exhaled air. This led to me passing out and effectively drowning before being found on the bottom and recovered to shore, where thankfully I was resuscitated.

By the nature of the hypoxic brain injury I suffered in that accident, I had frontal lobe damage and when I came round in hospital a memory that circled around every couple of minutes, like a proverbial goldfish, and I struggled to hold a thought. That memory cycle would improve over the following years, but there would always be a cognitive shortfall, that I would either learn to by-pass, or live with, usually a mixture of both. At the time, I didn't remember being married, how I'd got there, or what I'd been doing. So this is where the story begins, with a split second of misfortune, a near-death experience and a lifetime of consequences, but don't panic. In learning to face those consequences, to deal with them, and to rage against them, I managed to grasp a lifeline that has come to define the coming years.

On repatriation to the UK, I was lucky enough to get help from a psychologist, one Dr David Johnson, in learning to cope with the cognitive shortfall. One issue that would become a recurring theme over the ensuing years was controlling my mood. Due to the injury, the dark clouds that represented depression would sit, just on the horizon, and would encroach on life and recede again, depending on my ability to spot the encroachment and deal with it. Springsteen sang about, 'Darkness on the Edge of Town', if you get the drift? The principal method of doing this was to be physically active, or exercise. My two current outlets of kendo (Japanese fencing) and mountain biking, were deemed a little risky due to the possibility of further head trauma, however minor, so running was the fallback. I'd run for years, since my teenage years, actually, but never really competing, just running. Looking back on it now, I often wonder if I already used it as some sort of stress-relief valve, I can't really be sure. Now though, it became a first line of defence against mood swings, and I quickly got used to, 'suiting-up and heading out' whenever the vice tightened.

As time passed, the recovery went in swings and roundabouts, I lost my career, and the marriage, but over time rebuilt both, yet the proximity of depression never really changed, but my ability to at least keep it at bay did. This was largely due to the mechanisms Dr Johnson had instilled in me, that I now just considered an everyday part of life. This combined with running being the safety valve that has never failed me. There's no such thing as a 'bad' run really, they all help to a degree. Some are better than others, and some are truly sublime. It's 'mental downtime', where the electrical storm that my brain often finds itself in, in dealing with the everyday world, can be cleared and balance restored. What began as a necessity suddenly started to grow an internal logic of its own, with it becoming a bedrock for me, that never shifted, never failed, never shook. It is that base upon which I stand, every single day, and do so going forward. Byron Powell nailed it with the title of his legendary book, *Relentless Forward Progress*.

This was about the time that news started to spread from the US of a new version of racing, ominously (but impressively) called, 'ultra-racing'. Anniero's *Running Wild*, and the books of Jurek and Karnazes became required reading, and each book had a certain resonance with me. These were people who for different reasons and to different degrees, actually "got it". The realisation that what I considered a radical lifeline was actually pretty mainstream and widespread was truly intoxicating and comforting. What became obvious, as I started to delve deeper into that closeted world, or tribe, was common threads about why people chose to push their bodies to the very limits of endurance. It's not just elite athletes, either. Every weekend, normal people, in exponentially growing numbers, actively pursue the chance to find out the limits of their heart, head, and body. It's a community rich with stories (hence this book, I guess) from the very, "gods" of the sport, to those, "weekend warriors". We all have a tale to tell, and there's plenty of time on the trail to share them. It's spawned countless films and documentaries, a plethora of books, websites and research and an entire counter culture, with its own logic, structure and creed.

Alongside the hype, the burgeoning marketplace with all the merchandise and gear, and the continued self-therapy, came the races that continue to define my 'rage against age' (I'm 52 now) and reaffirmed my survival. It's how I like to remind myself of the events that sought to define my life, and what I do by way of revenge and to celebrate a life well lived. What also came was the friendships and connections that are a true treasure and source of joy. People you haven't spoken to in years suddenly cross your path in the middle of nowhere and run with you for miles, full of stories, and joint revelry in the sheer joy of just running on the face of this earth. Entirely, in my experience, non judgmental. And wholly supportive from the elites down, and vice versa.

It's taken me to some great places (the Kerry Way Ultra Lite, in Ireland for my 50th), to the limits of what I believed I could do (73 miles across Scotland for the Great Glen Ultra, in sixteen hours, nine minutes and fifty two seconds). Am I done? Not by a long stretch, pardon the pun. There are plenty of places to go, races to race, people to meet, or revisit, and life to reaffirm. Many of the people I know are kindred spirits. They know where the clouds are laying in wait, but how to keep them there, and that builds a strong camaraderie. Some do it because of the jointly held, burgeoning desire to continually test their own limits, or those of others, or just because they have that deep need not to quit. There are some wonderful memories, some fantastic plans, some genuine dreams, and more than its fair share of glorious craziness (Barkley anyone?). But at the first, and at the last are the connections.

'Normal' folk, think we're utterly certifiable. If you're reading this and are one of those, rest assured ultra-runners hold the reciprocal view. I mean, what did you do today to remind yourself, and celebrate the fact, that you're alive?

Ultra-runners. We are one. We are legion.

How far is, 'far', anyway?

Paul Pickford

The last night of a four-day non-stop 214-mile race across Scotland was the darkest point in my running career.

Having been force-fed cheese and beans on toast, had my clothes changed by my family and slept for about an hour and a half, I was ready to continue. This was after spending the previous five or six hours hallucinating due to sleep deprivation. Hallucinations that I can still see and wonder why on earth such random things popped into my head and stayed there. Inside my head I had an old Asian lady perched on a set of IKEA shelves shouting negative comments and a pack of dogs running around in circles!

The three guys I was with were going too fast for me, as my feet were in bits, so I had to tell them to go on and leave me to get on with it on my own. My wife and daughter, who were crewing, pulled up alongside me to check I was ok. I told them to leave me and go on ahead. This was the hardest thing I had done because I was feeling mentally lost and adrift. I was at an all-time low and could not see myself at the finish.

Deep down I knew I had to feel comfortable being uncomfortable to get it done. My wife and daughter drove off down the road and flashed the car lights where the trail went off-road and up into the hills. I refocused myself, told myself that there was only one person that could get this done and started moving forward. Off I set on my own, upset that I couldn't keep up with Ray, with whom I had spent most of the previous three days, sharing the highs and lows of the long-distance race, but I was determined to try to catch up with them. After a few hours of being alone and digging deeper than I ever thought possible, I eventually caught up with them. Pretty much crying with joy and feeling stronger, I had beaten the self-doubt that had been in my head for hours.

Together as a team, we cajoled each other, leading a section at a time, setting a pace, joining in the map-reading discussions, waiting for each other. We reached the finish line together with an hour and a half to spare on an overall 100-hour cut-off to complete the entire length of the Southern Upland Way, with its 25,000ft of ascent – Everest is 29,029ft!!

Seeing and crossing the finish line had me in tears. Not only had I achieved the goal but the pain and suffering could finally stop. Even now, when I look at the finishers' buckle, I get a sense that on any other day I could have failed and I am grateful for all the training I had put in.

That was this year's adventure. However, running didn't come easily to me. My running started in 2001 at the age of 29, pushing 19 stone and about to be on prescription drugs for blood pressure. The doctor suggested exercise and gave me a chance to avoid being on tablets for the rest of my life. I had a friend that ran and had told me stories about the 'Tough Guy' races. I felt I had to give this a go but it was a major goal with the lure of a medal at the finish giving me the determination to start training.

I entered my first race, the New Forest 10-mile, feeling confident standing at the start line wearing brand new shorts and T-shirt. I finished the race in over 2 hours with lots of chaffing and 'jogger's nipple'! I learnt lessons, continued to lose weight and get fitter. I knew I wanted to challenge myself more, both mentally and physically. Three Tough Guy races came and went, some very tough times when everything hurt, but the bling made up for it. It was all about the medals. Each one was a manifestation of my determination, toil and achievement. I have never displayed my medals, at the beginning they used to hang on the hook behind my dressing gown – a constant reminder of everything I had achieved and what I was capable of when I needed a perk. Now they live in a shoebox under the bed. I don't need to look at them so often nowadays.

In 2005, I was watching Ben Fogle running the Marathon des Sables (MdS) on TV with my wife and saying "if he can do it then so can I". She called my bluff, "go on then" – having a very young family and hardly any money I wrote a begging letter to my boss who put down the deposit to enable me to register, and fundraised with a local charity to make sure I couldn't back out. I was in shock and this now scared the life out of me, but I wanted to know if I could do it. Scared stiff, I entered my first marathon – the Isle of Wight – not the flattest but to finish it felt amazing, although I struggled to walk back to the car after getting off the ferry. Then my first double marathon which, although it was very slow and physically painful, gave me the confidence that it is possible to complete the double day on the MdS. Lots of slow training miles, getting very comfortable with running solo, running in all weathers and terrain, running once the children were in bed, working on nutrition and fundraising followed.

2007, the Marathon des Sables, an amazing running experience, physically exhausting and I considered it the very edge of human capability. It was emotional receiving daily messages from my family and friends through the week, most messages would make me cry. On day 5 – the rest day – hearing that one of the competitors had passed away in his sleep the night before brought home just what a crazy adventure this was. On the last day and the final finish line, I didn't want to cross the line, didn't want the adventure to be over so I sat on the last sand dune, in sight of the finish line, contemplating what I had achieved and where I had come from.

Having thought that I had now achieved my running goal and could stop and rest on my laurels, I found myself wondering just how far the mind and body could go. My weight was down, as was the blood pressure and the training felt good, but I needed another challenge to concentrate on as I missed the thrill of having something to train for. This led to me entering the Grand Union Canal Race, an iconic 145-mile non-stop footrace from Birmingham to London. I had already run the 'toughest footrace on earth', I thought it would be a walk in the park. However, very little training and a lot of complacency led to a spectacular fail at around 85 miles, where my mind told my body to quit. It was the first time I had dealt with this mental incapacity to understand what was happening and stay in control.

The demons of failing to complete this race preyed heavy in my mind for years afterwards. In a race I would never give it my all, I would always finish a run with a little in reserve. I would finish mid-pack, enjoying my races but always making sure I could carry on just a bit further. It wasn't until 2015 that it occurred to me: I could go back! To return I knew I had to plan and to train properly. I upped the game by volunteering as a marshal on Centurion 100-mile events so I could see the pain and suffering in real-time. The courage and determination evident, more so, in the mid-to-back of the runner pack as they were out on the course for a substantially longer time than the front-runners.

2015 meant my first attempt at a nonstop 100 miles. With amazing support from good friends, both as crew and buddy running, I achieved a 24:40 finish. Finish times have never really been important to me, just staying ahead of cut-offs is always enough, I like to be thought of as "a completer and not a competitor". The feeling of finishing this was one of incredible happiness and, for the first time, a deep wonder: could I get under 24 hours?

I was beginning to understand that after completing these long runs the feeling of satisfaction, accomplishment and self-belief is immense, however, there is also a void which can bring you down and leave you feeling adrift.

2016, Centurion Thames Path hundred. Having trained hard with back-to-back runs most weekends I had the aim of completing it in sub 24-hours. With the support of friends who didn't give up on me and helped me when times got tough, nudging me along when I spent too long at checkpoints, random conversations that helped to pass the time. Always moving forward, I achieved a sub-24-hour 100 miles – a running milestone. Once again, sometime afterwards there was a void in my life that needed filling.

In 2016 I entered the draw for a place on the Grand Union Canal Race 2017, thinking, "it's a draw, I won't get in first time", famous last words… 2017, Grand Union Canal: *The Rematch*! Mentally prepared, as much as anyone could, I was focusing on seeing myself crossing the finish line. Concentrating on positive thoughts and being physically prepared. So many training miles and recce runs, one of which involved my wife going to an overnight conference in Birmingham, dropping me off just outside Northampton and picking me up the next day at the M25.

I had an amazing crew in preparation for this, including my wife and several experienced ultra-runners I had met at other events that had become very good friends. They knew how important this was to me, it was the best chance I had.

At about mile 120 with so much self-doubt in my physical ability, probably due to fatigue and trying to stay positive, it would have been easy to quit. However, the desire to push through and complete was so strong. I was more scared at this stage of having to come back and try again so I kept pushing on, eventually finishing the race in just over 40 hours. I had done it! Quite literally putting the demons to bed. It wasn't the bling, which was great, it was the knowledge that if you really want something: focus and train, then it can be achieved.

As I have understood more about how to train for these events, the training became part of family life: a day out in the car sometimes involved me getting out of the car miles away from home and running back; 'run to work Friday' has been and still is a thing (run to work at "oh my goodness it's dark" o'clock, then after work running the long way – up to 30 miles – home) to set up the weekend and it doesn't interrupt family life too much.

The winter of 2017 was a particularly large void. I always feel a little lost if not training for something and experienced the 'black dog' which seems to follow me after any of these events. I started to look for another challenge which would see how far I could push myself mentally and physically. I found the GB Ultra Scotland, a non-stop 214-mile run the length of the Southern Upland Way. It was the first time on this route so a new challenge all around.

I paid my money and immediately went for a run, thinking "what on earth have I done", but knowing that I now had a goal to aim for. For me, everything seems easier in life if I have a personal goal to aim for; work pressures don't seem so bad and I seem to be happier in myself.

Training for the Southern Upland Way meant another Centurion 100 miler to test my mind, body and nutrition. No running buddies on this one and a support crew of one. This race focused on trying to overcome personal negativity, accepting it would be difficult and a good test for being self-sufficient in Scotland a couple of months later. This was a great experience and finishing in just over 25 hours allowed me to believe that the race across Scotland was achievable. After being driven home on that Sunday morning, and in true training style, straight back out and running/stumbling a quick 5k, well I had another 114 miles to go…

For me, running and training has become an important, positive part of my life and my mental health. Running is never about competing with anyone but myself, it's not just about the distance, terrain or the weather. For me, it's about the 'rested mind' positive mental health that comes with distance running.

A positive side effect of my running journey is the fantastic feeling I've discovered from helping others achieve their goals. From a 5k parkrun to an ultra-marathon, supporting others to reach their goals is better than medals for me now. Running has taught me that if you want something and are prepared to work for it you can achieve a healthy lifestyle, both in body and mind.

So, what does the future hold? 2019 brings my first attempt at the North Downs Way 100-mile Ultra; spending time discovering more local trails; and encouraging others to enjoy long distance trails and mud runs just as I do.

Paul Pickford, 46, married father of two from Portchester, Hampshire, UK

Sheila Aavilesc

I started running when I was 10 years old. I did track and field. I've raced the Matterhorn Ultraks, climbing 3,883 metres in Zermatt, Switzerland. I didn't train specifically for this race. This meant I suffered a lot as I had only prepared for shorter distances. The race went ok and I finished in third place.

I run four days a week. I also do other training such as cycling and strength training. I love running as it makes me feel free and exhausted. When running, I disconnect from society. I love being in the moment and connecting with nature. Running has taught me values like fighting, sacrificing and perseverance to reach my goals. In the future I would like to do ultra trails. Next season I would like to do more mediation races.

I'm from a village in Catolina in Spain called Santa Margarita. I'm 25 years old and I'm a personal trainer too. I'm studying for a Master's degree in training elite athletes.

Oliver Smith

Hi, I'm Oli, a 35 year-old living with my young family in South Wales. I've always loved the outdoors, but I first started running in 2009, taking someone's place in the Great South Run on 24 hours' notice. I didn't know what to expect, I knew no-one taking part and I was tired from a tough game of rugby (and a couple of drinks) the day before. To cut a long (well, 80-minute) story short, I started off trying to compete with anyone who was near me, but quickly realised this was a futile mistake and after about 5 miles settled in to a routine of just trying to high-five as many supporters as possible. The two memories that stick with me were the relief at finishing, and not being able to get back in my car afterwards (6ft 4 + VW Polo problems).

Fast forward almost 10 years and my rugby days were coming to an end, I had two young kids in tow and time for outdoor fun was limited to the odd day in the mountains or weekend by the sea. As I'd always been very active in my twenties, I'd never had time to stop and reflect on the wider benefits of an outdoor lifestyle. With the benefit of hindsight, I realised I was missing not only the physical fitness, but also the cathartic aspects of sport, the endorphin release, the shared experiences, embracing nature and the benefits of a well-earned rest afterwards. Having lived by the coast for the majority of my life, I'd previously thrown myself into surfing to unwind from work and life pressures.

In 2014 we moved to Cardiff, so the previous pre-
and post-work surfs were relegated to a couple of
days a year when the conditions aligned. I started
running to and from work a couple of days a week,
then a couple of years later signed up to the
Cardiff Half Marathon to raise money for a local
charity I was involved with. I was subsequently
asked to run the October version for another
charity, and ended up dressed as a banana.

Fast forward another six months to Spring 2017
and I was running in my first '1/2 Ultra', the
RunWalkCrawl Vale of Glamorgan 19-miler. I'd
done no formal training for it, although had racked
up a total of 100 miles in January as part of an
office bet. It was the toughest 3.5 hours of
exercise I'd ever done, but I met some
inspirational people on the way round, who all
appeared to be enjoying it much more than I was
(certainly towards the end!).

Anyway, after a summer of fell running in some
stunning South Wales locations, I decided to have
a crack at the Gower 50, with a good friend, once
again raising money for charity.

I thought I knew Gower intimately from surf and
camping trips over the years, but this was an
extraordinary race, 12.5 hours of rain interspersed
with a few rays of sunshine around a beautiful
coastline. My poor navigational skills forced me to
come out of my shell and talk to the other runners,
once again an inspirational bunch, and it was
these interactions that really made the event

something truly special. The support and team work from strangers was incredible. The half marathons I'd previously run had a great atmosphere, but the underlying reason for the majority of runners is to set a PB, or see how fast they can run it, rather than to enjoy, savour and complete it.

I expected the Gower 50 to showcase breathtaking scenery whilst giving me a total physical and mental beating, what I didn't expect was the joy of the friendships forged on the trails. The distance of the race forces you to run at a much slower pace, and for me I got a totally new and unexpected experience. It was the first time I'd crossed a finish line not absolutely drained from my exertions, I didn't have any blisters, and although pretty stiff, I was back coaching mini-rugby the following day.

My time of 12.5 hours was 4 hours slower than the fastest, but still enough to put me in the top quarter of entrants. I loved it and the bug was caught.

Over Christmas my foot started playing up, and I became increasingly frustrated at not being able to get outside and run. The pain was excruciating, so I went to the physio to be told it's chronic and will hurt like hell but that light training should be fine. I was over the moon so started running with a few local running clubs (through friends I'd made in the 50), and got involved helping to set up a new looped trail running event in the Brecon Beacon foothills (trying to a develop a sustainable, more inclusive ultra event for all levels of runner). I now felt less like an imposter in a new sporting environment, and I started asking around for new events to enter in 2018…

Someone suggested the Brecon Beacons 50 miler (SW50) on the 22nd/23rd June with circa 3,000m of climbing through the South Wales mountains. Having recently completed my first 50 miler, and once again with a superb cause to raise money for (Oshi's World, a local children's charity), I thought that I should go for the 100-mile (6,400m+ elevation) version instead to give me the best chance of persuading donors to part with their money. My decision to run the SW100 was greeted with an eye roll by Catrin (my long-suffering wife), but it seemed like a good idea at the time…

My training regime kicked off in earnest, and with three months to go before the big day I was intending to try and get 60+ miles a week in, fitting in training amongst family and work responsibilities. I very quickly realised that I wasn't up to those levels of training, tried to blot out the fact that the race was looming, and was only managing a maximum of 15 miles a week. I'd also hoped to join the race recce runs in the lead up to the event, but missed them all due to family commitments.

Once May hit, I realised I was hugely underprepared, but my foot was no longer giving me grief, and I was feeling relatively fit. With a significant amount of money already raised I realised I had no choice but to carry on. At this stage I was justifying my chances of completing based on the fact I was relatively comfortable on the 50, and that it's only twice the distance – completely disregarding the fact there was a literal Everest's worth of climbing in the 100 too. I reckoned I could do it in around 24 hours based on the fact I didn't collapse over the line on finishing the 50. What an idiot.

Two weeks before the 100 I had my first reality check when lucky enough to join some of the local MWD runners on their training run for the 50-mile event. We did the last 25 miles of the route, and I found out that not only was my endurance fitness woeful, but my navigational skills were dubious at best in daylight, and non-existent at night. The SW100 sets off at 7pm on the Friday, so I'd have at least one night running and navigating in the dark. I had been rudely awakened.

I then had half-term in France with the family, managing one 3-mile run with Catrin and a few loops of the ferry on the way back. There was one week to go.

My final-week preparations were interspersed with juggling work, kids and an extension on the house. I didn't have all the compulsory kit, I didn't have a running vest to carry it all, I couldn't get my Garmin to work properly, and I didn't start packing until I'd finished work at 4pm on the Friday! This gave me an hour to help the builders move some rubbish, grab a bite to eat, and get over to the registration for 5pm (luckily only 3 miles from my front door). The best thing about my lack of prep was the fact I was so busy I couldn't dwell on it.

It was at registration when it sunk in that I had bitten off more – way, way more – than I could chew. There were around 60 competitors for the 100-miler, and all of them looked like the gnarled, sinewy experienced ultra-athletes of the magazines and adverts! I luckily knew a friendly face on the registration desk who calmed me a bit, and then I had about an hour to pack and repack my 30-litre rucksack and work out which pair of boardies to wear.

It wasn't until we congregated at the start line that the nerves kicked in. Having played competitive team sport for most of my life I was familiar with the pre-match feeling, but this was the first time I was doing something way out of my comfort zone on my own (since the 2009 Great South Run, and I was hungover then so it didn't feel quite so bad!). I have never experienced nerves like it. It was partly due to the support I'd had from friends and family and the sponsorship raised, which gave me an overwhelming sense of dread as I knew I'd let a lot of people down if I couldn't complete the race. The other aspect was the unknown. I've never pushed my mind or body through anything like this, and my lack of preparation meant I had no idea how on earth I would respond to the exhaustion, exertion, navigation, and general peril of the run. Luckily I didn't have too long to think about it, and the hooter was sounded and we were off.

I stayed at the back, where the sedentary pace was relaxing, and got chatting with a few of my fellow runners. The joys of an ultra meant that I spent the next 16 hours with the same bunch – Steve, Gary and Rachel, so we got to know each other well, taking turns leading and keeping spirits high. I found out that they'd all previously attempted the SW100, but either had to pull out through injury or had not made the cut-offs. But the weather was clear and warm so we had a beautiful sunset and sunrise to ease into the first half of the route. By mile 40 I was still in high spirits, but we were by now heading into waterfall country, in the foothills of the Brecon Beacons. The route was perfect, heading up and down ravines along with rolling countryside. The ominous presence of the Pen y Fan mountain range could also be felt, as the shadows loomed some 15 or so miles to the north-west. I'd made sure I was regularly eating and drinking, with cold pizza the most prized meal on my menu and my three-litre Aquapac constantly filled up at the 12 mile-ish feed stations.

There were a couple of wrong turns (mainly due to my over-enjoyment of the mountain views) and by the time we reached the Taff Trail at the foot of Corn Du our caravan of four had dwindled to two, with just Rachel and I remaining. The mountains were teaming with folks out enjoying the sunshine and racing in other mountain events (The Fan Dance was in full swing by mid-morning). It was great chatting with all those out enjoying the fresh air and spectacular views, but a rude awakening awaited me at the summit of Pen y Fan.

I had taken a moment to catch my breath and reflect on the journey so far. By this time I'd been awake for coming up to 30 hours and racing for over 18 hours, it was hard and dusty underfoot but I was happy and (surprisingly!) still enjoying myself. There were hundreds on the peak though, and I longed for the stillness that had accompanied us for the first overnight leg. As I called to Rachel to get us moving a lovely little dog ran past, wrapping my legs in its lead. As I bent down to free myself and continue on, the owner retracted the lead, causing it to scythe into me, ripping wounds into the back of my legs. More on this later, as at this point I barely felt a thing, and hurried after Rachel to get the second half of the ultra back underway.

We had a break to refuel at the top of Cribyn, I tended my legs, ate half a pizza (delicious – so good for morale too!) and sun-screened up before we got on our way. The next 8 miles or so along the ridgeline is amongst my favourite memories. Rachel scampered away, agreeing to rendezvous at the Talybont Reservoir, so I had my first caffeine gel and got my headphones out. For the next hour and a half I was flying, singing at the top of my lungs and running amidst stunning scenery! The sky was so clear that navigation was easy, and I cruised in to the Talybont feed station feeling revitalised and pretty confident. It was here I bumped into a few of the SW50 runners, three of whom had retired, through heat stroke, injury and fatigue. I swiftly came down from my high – the previous 60 miles had started to take its toll. My feet and knees by this time were falling apart, I was dehydrated and had been awake pushing 36 hours. The one redeeming aspect was the fact there were only 40 miles left to go, and the significant peaks were now behind us…

… the next leg started with a climb to the 550m pinnacle of Tor y Foel, passing a couple more of the SW50 competitors on the way up. The overtaking didn't spur me on, and as the descent began I was in the midst of a physical and mental low. My knees had packed up, and it was excruciating going downhill. I could no longer run! I nabbed a sturdy branch from a nearby tree to use as a crutch, and rued the fact that I'd not bothered to learn how to use the walking poles I'd picked up a few days before (they were still nestled unused in the boot of my car). It was here I told Rachel to head on without me, as she was still in top spirits and in much better shape than me.

The route down to the next feed station was pretty easy, and relatively flat, and I spied a couple of other runners in the distance, which buoyed my spirits. Dusk was falling as I arrived in Trefil, and in between stuffing my face with super noodles I got chatting to another seasoned ultra runner,

Kevin, who was on his third attempt at the SW100. His motivation was startling – he had spent the spring recceing the course to give himself the utmost chance of success, and had probably covered the entire route four or five times in training. His upbeat outlook rubbed off on me, and I set off alongside him for the second night of the race.

We only had about 25 miles left, but I was struggling to keep up. We were now running through villages, past pubs with patrons spilling outside and cheering us on. As the night drew in the terrain became a vast moonscape, dusty, rocky and hostile. We were well in front of the cut-off times, but it was here I was really doubting my ability to complete – I was struggling to keep up with Kevin's small group and was becoming disorientated. I felt a sharp pain in my right foot and remember persevering for a mile or so before realising I needed to get rid of what appeared to be a large stone in my shoe. I didn't want to sit down for fear of cramping up, so, balancing on one leg, I managed to get my shoe off. I glanced at my sock, and saw it was covered in blood – it dawned on me that what must have been a huge blister on the ball of my foot had just popped. Taking off my shoe was the worst thing to have done, as I now had to put it back on, try and lace it with shaking fingers, then catch up with the disappearing head torches on the hillside. This was my darkest moment yet. My whole body hurt, I was starting to hallucinate and each step was pure agony. It was the middle of the night, I was about 30 hours in (awake for over 42 hours) and I had at least another 6 hours left. I was almost willing myself to fall and get a debilitating injury so I could pull out and end the ordeal without letting down Oshi's World and all who had supported me.

For some reason I carried on. There was no epiphany, no startling realisation. It dawned on me that my body, whilst feeling completely broken, was capable of finishing. It had become a battle against myself. I didn't have the energy to dig around in my backpack for headphones, so I began an internal monologue of just counting the steps I was taking. This culminated in about two hours where I was incapable of counting higher than '2', so I had to endure the repetition of my brain saying '1', '2', '1', '2'… over and over again. Incredibly this tactic started to work, and I managed to keep up with Kevin and the others who were with him. The relief at reaching the final feed station in Caerphilly was fantastic. I even managed to joke with the volunteers who were manning it, although their visible shock at how atrocious I looked scared me slightly. I took myself to the toilet to wash my hands and face, and scarcely recognised the hollow face looking back at me.

This prompted me into rallying the troops for the final leg, and at 3am, after a 10-minute rest, we were off again. Unknown to me, the 10 miles back to Cardiff included three more big hills, and about 500m more climbing. The finish line was within touching distance, but it took a further 4 hours to reach it – not even a second stunning sunrise could rouse me from my despondent mood that had taken over. The child in me came out, and I was constantly asking Kevin "are we there yet?"! When we hit the final mile they suggested we finish with a flourish and jog it in. I sent them off on their own, as I didn't have it in me to increase the pace of my shuffling, but they stayed with me until the last. Absolutely fantastic folks.

Catrin and the kids had been following my progress online, and they were alarmed to see how much I was struggling and how far behind my unrealistic schedule I was. She and the kids headed to the finish line for breakfast and to wait for me to arrive. I stumbled over the line at 7.30am, 36.5 hours and 104 miles after setting off. I was in 29th place, coming in ahead of the last remaining entrant by about 5 minutes. No-one else finished.

What were my feelings on crossing the line? I didn't have any, no relief, no joy, nothing. I was devoid of emotion. I collected my medal, thanked Kevin and the rest of our finishing collective for their overwhelming help in guiding me through the latter stages, and headed to the car. I was in such a state that I thought the car was wobbling like jelly – it was then I started incoherently giggling to myself!

The immediate aftermath was tough. Catrin manipulated me into the house and into the bath. I then had to use surgical scissors to remove my socks and calf compressors (they had both fused into the cuts made by the dog lead). I won't go into the extent of the other wounds I'd developed, but various ointments were applied by the gallon. By 8.30am I was collapsed in bed. I woke at about 1pm starving, and was treated to lunch in bed, before dozing for the rest of the day. Physically I was broken, but the sleep had restored my brain and the relief in being able to think and function was almost euphoric! I had to wear flip flops and use walking sticks for the next two weeks, and go on a course of antibiotics for the now heavily infected wounds in my calf, but I had finished, and I now look back with immense fondness at the achievement and those friendships I made on route.

Within a week I was back on the bike, within two I was back jogging, albeit very tentatively. I finally started to feel proud of the achievement and the money I'd been able to raise. The worst aspect was being so physically broken at the end that I had to go a couple of weeks without running, and the infected wounds kept me out of the water for almost a month.

The biggest lesson I took away was that it's easier to be happy when you strip everything away – by the end of the 104 miles all I needed was food, shelter and sleep to get me on an even keel. For 36.5 hours I'd worried about nothing more than putting one foot in front of the other, all other stresses evaporated.

I was also overwhelmed by what we had all managed to endure, and six months on I still marvel at how the rest of the runners I got to know over the course of the run managed to stay so positive and happy throughout. The kindness of strangers and awe-inspiring humanity shown by the other competitors and volunteers has stuck with me long after the event finished.

Nikki Yeo

I started running in 2007 after I had completed the Moonwalk Marathon with my best friend. This involved walking 26.2 miles at night around London with women, all raising money for a breast cancer charity. We trained well and I found the event ticked all the boxes and we got round in a very respectable 6 hours 45 minutes. So, I thought I would give running a go and started with 5 mins on the treadmill! At that time I could not imagine running outside, in public with other people. I was far too self-conscious and worried what people might think.

Inspired by an article I read whilst sat by the pool in Corfu in the summer of 2007 in which comedian Jo Brand talked about a Women's only 5k in Hyde Park, I signed up for my first race – the Hydroactive Women's 5K. I thought if Jo Brand can do it so can I. My husband and two boys came along to cheer me on and I ran the whole thing in 33 mins and I loved it.

I decided to go for longer distances, I liked the ability to dial into a pace and relax. From here I progressed to my first marathon in 2010. I loved the training and the race as it gave me space from my then youngish family – aged 13 and 10 at the time. I ran when they were at clubs or at school and the freedom of being outside and seeing, hearing and smelling things like flowers and cut grass and mud gave me a natural balance and a level of calm. The marathon distance suited me and my pace, and I loved the discovery of new routes and what worked as fuel and what didn't!

At my first marathon I was excited and nervous and took way too many photos in the first half and then crashed and burnt in the second. But, what a feeling. I ran 4 hours 48 and it took me about two days to process what I had done. It took me a few years of marathon running to think of myself as a runner and to realise quite how much I needed running in my life, to balance the highs and the lows and the stresses of family life! I enjoy seeing my body change, pushing my boundaries. I am not at the front of the pack or the last, in fact I am pretty much always in the middle! I began to add parkrun into my running from October 2012 and discovered a community of like-minded people who loved to run and chat. I was hooked and began to add parkun to my long runs. I think of parkrun as my first running club!

In January 2013 we, as a family, had a tragic event: my brother-in-law Neil chose to end his life.

He was in his mid-30s and the trail of devastation that was immediate and still ripples is like nothing I have ever experienced. Trying to make sense of this and to explain as best you can to two teenage boys what had happened was hard. The natural protection of your closest family and friends kicks in and the word suicide becomes something real and something that I wanted to research and look into and see what I could do to help others. I went along to Samaritans training and also ran lots of miles with no agenda, just processing. It was something that happened to others, not to close family and helping my sister I found myself in places doing and seeing things that quite frankly are hard to digest. It is almost as if suicide is suddenly on the agenda, an option and a terrifying one that makes you want to talk all the time about mental health and the importance of listening, really listening and asking people if they are ok. My social media timelines are often full of posts from the many wonderful organisations that we can turn to for help. I will never stop sharing and I believe the more we talk and share the better equipped we become in helping others and ourselves.

I ran Brighton Marathon with Neil's photo on my back and that was one of the most emotional runs that I have ever done; he chose to stop and I wanted to carry on. I crossed the line having cried most of the way around and spent an hour in a St John's Ambulance – I was on my second course of antibiotics!

It was after this that I became fascinated with ultra running and started chatting to runners on Twitter. I was in awe of runners doing the MdS and other crazy races. I lurked and soaked up all the advice. I went along to volunteer with the wonderful Centurion Running at the North Downs Way 50. I chose the last aid station at mile 42 deliberately so that I could see for myself what sort of runners there were and what state they were in!! I loved every minute of it and was pleased to see that there were mostly normal runners like me.

That was that and I went on to do a local 50k at Portsmouth Coastal in 5 hours 40, followed by the Downslink Ultra. I took the Downslink easy and added walk breaks of a minute after 10 miles. I was amazed that with this strategy and just enjoying the trail I was able to go past other runners. I finished this in 7 hours 21. Suddenly I was out discovering trails and hills and felt empowered to be on them more often than not on my own, which I found incredibly humbling. I love the feeling of being outside, with a pack on with everything I need and just following paths and climbing over wooden gates, passing cows and sheep and constantly pushing that bit further. The inner calm that comes during and after a run is addictive; my husband often says "just go for a run!" I enjoy running both on my own and with others. The sense of community that can be found in the ultra running world is wonderful, people share advice and help each other out and the chatter is the best!

I have only clocked up eight or so ultras with a couple of NDW50s, which I love. I break these up checkpoint to checkpoint and the first one I was happy to finish – 11 hours 40 with a 13-hour cut-off! The next time was 10 hours 54. The longest to date is Race to the Stones – 100km in 14 hours 20 minutes. I trained for it with a friend who sadly had to drop out due to injury. My husband then decided to come along and cheer me on at the aid stations. I was so grateful as I was a bundle of nerves and managed to fall over just after the start! I got chatting to a fellow parkrunner about 20 miles in and we ended up sort of running the rest together. I loved the feeling of powering on and despite being sick at about mile 55, I loved it! I was determined to finish before it was dark and I did. I was amazed with what I had achieved, a wife, a mother and a primary school librarian and I had just run 62 miles and I wasn't rubbish!

I have had one attempt at a 100-mile race and that ended at mile 62 somewhere in Kent. It was August, hot and humid and I was having a bad irritable bowel syndrome (IBS) flare-up which caused me to be sick from mile 22, which is unusual for me. I couldn't keep anything down and despite the efforts of the volunteers and a complete change of clothes I knew it was game over.

That was 2018 and this year (2019) I am signed up for another 100, this one again with Centurion but the SDW, not the NDW. I have been sorting out the stomach issues and am ready to give it another go! In a strange way I feel having a DNF at this distance makes me feel even more part of the community.

My family mostly think I am bonkers as do my friends and colleagues. I feel running long distances balances me and keeps the mental health mania at bay. I run most days, I like the consistency. On average it is about five times a week, always with a parkun and always a long run. I run on holiday as it is the perfect way to really see a new place. I work things through when I am running, I lose myself in my thoughts. I cry and laugh in the middle of woods with deer for company. I sing, badly, along paths that cannot be seen from the roads and pavements and I am grateful every day for the ability to run. I come from a split family, as does my husband, and this itself comes with many complications. Running is not complicated, running and chatting are good for the soul – sole to soul running, I say.

The anniversary of my brother-in-law's suicide is 30th January so very close by. He jumped off the 100ft cliff at Peacehaven, which you can see as you run Brighton and is a shocking time in our life, and to have been thrown into it immediately, driving to get my sister who was in Brighton and dealing with the coroner, mortuary etc was, well, sort of surreal. I have run marathons for the Samaritans and also Grassroots Suicide to help raise awareness and end the stigma of suicide. My timeline is full of mental health wellbeing posts that I will never apologise for sharing. It affected both my boys and still does – the ultimate question – how does someone get to that place where the only option they can see is to end their own life? To choose to do so?

I have a few ultras booked and hope to maybe better my times but mostly I enter because of the personal challenge and the epic routes. I think it is important to do something that scares you, that takes you out of your comfort zone and for that is running in fields and trails, coming face to face with cows and horses in the day and at night. I never regret a run, despite faffing about sometimes before I go out of the door! I like the kit and the laying out of the kit. I still get nervous and am learning too control this. The ultra running world is a wonderful place, the chatter, the slightly bonkers element of it all, full of all kinds of people and most of which you have no idea what they do other than their running CV! It is the best way to work things through in your head, whether alone or with music or a podcast. It is therapy, mental and physical, and if I can do it, so can anyone!

Mario Frucci

I love this idea, and since I have yet to compete in an ultra (first ultra takes place on 18th May of this year) I may not have the experience you are looking for, nonetheless I will give it a go...

As an athlete for most of my life I grew up playing hockey, however, I have always had a pair of running shoes and would train in my off-season by participating in camps and other off-ice (dryland) training programs. I would try to go out for runs with very little training in endurance sports and always returned disappointed with my time or distance. Almost every time I would get shin splints, knocking me out for a few days, then repeating those same mistakes over and over through high school and into my early twenties while I was going to college in Central Minnesota.

In February of 2018 I decided that I needed a lifestyle change. One that was positive, challenging, and would require discipline in order to get back in shape, and most importantly, avoid having to go get a new belt and ANOTHER new pair of jeans. I really needed to get in shape. I started running by time. First, for 15 minutes, with a 5-minute walk, followed by another 15 minutes of what I called hjogging [HEE-YOGGING (hike-jogging)] on the trails at the state park near my home in Central Minnesota. Mind you, this was February in Minnesota, and I refused to run inside on a treadmill. I wanted to feel it, the cold, the pain, all of it. I kept at it, and by April I was running for 45 minutes without stopping and I realised that I was running 4 miles per run, running every other day to avoid injury and risking any type of setback.

On 11 May, 2018, I set out on a normal evening run. I hadn't decided how far I was going to run that day, I just wanted to run until I felt like it. I was on a bike trail loop that was 1.1 miles long. I kept running around and around and around until I realised I was going farther than I ever had before. By the time I was done, I had completed 11.1 miles in 1:45:00. I was flabbergasted! How on Earth did I do that?! At that point it was my longest run, and I knew that with the right training, I could do a half marathon but not just any half marathon, I wanted to run a race on trails. Even today I prefer trails to roads. I signed up for my first trail race in late May of '18 and on 20 October, 2018 I completed my first trail half marathon, the Harder N' Hell Half Marathon as part of the Wild Duluth Races here in Duluth, Minnesota. The race runs along the Superior Hiking Trail, a rugged single-track hiking trail that runs along the north shore of Lake Superior. Where I live in Central Minnesota, there are not many hills or rugged terrain like the race course so I had to improvise by running the same hills up and down, run stairs, and was constantly doing squats in my office to prep my legs for the nearly 4,000ft of elevation change on the race course. Mid-summer, in July, we got a puppy, which really put a damper in my training as a lot of my free time was spent with my wife and new mini Aussie puppy, aptly named, Minnie :). I was running longer miles, fewer days than I had early on in my training, but I kept my training as a high priority.

I finished that race as a top-20 male, in 2:45:22, almost 15 minutes faster than my goal of 3 hours. After the race was done I was so emotional, I let it all out, and cried my eyes out. After returning to the hotel and spending time with my family, I felt fine. Like totally fine. I was frustrated. I wanted to feel it. I wanted to be SUPER sore, and feel like I accomplished something spectacular. I did do something spectacular to a lot of people in my circle, but I knew by the end of the day, I needed to do an ultra.

Currently I am training for my first ultramarathon. On 18 May, 2019 I will compete in my first trail ultra (50K), the Superior Spring Trail Race held in Lutsen, Minnesota on the same trail, the Superior Hiking Trail, just 125 miles or so north of my first trail race. I have started training specifically for that race by running more hills, and continuing to push myself on my weekend long runs, which aren't exactly necessary for running a half marathon. I try to run four days a week, with back-to-back long runs on the weekends. Being in Minnesota, as I write this the actual air temperature is one degree above zero, with a low temp of 10 BELOW tonight (the forecast next week looks pretty grim as well). This makes training difficult, but not impossible. It's simply one more obstacle that running has taught me how to 'embrace the suck' and go for it. Whatever it is, go for it 100%.

What I enjoy most about running is the ability to let everything else fade away, and focus solely on my training and improving my endurance, pushing my body to the limits. I am almost 30 pounds lighter than when I started running almost a year ago, and I continually hear from friends that I'm killing it, which is fuel for me to keep hammering and pushing myself to new unprecedented heights. As far as my mental health goes, I am happier, and more focused when I am at work. I am able to focus on the task at hand with much greater confidence in myself and what I am capable of. running has taught me so much: patience, perseverance, gratitude, and I feel balance in my life for the first time in a long time. I don't have the energy to lash out at things that used to make my blood boil, because I need that energy later on in the day to kick my training plan's arse. Or on the flip side, if I run in the morning, I used all that excess energy during my run, and expending any of that remaining energy in a way that doesn't maintain balance is simply not worth it.

I love running, it has been one of the best things that has ever happened to me, to be a runner. One day, God willing, I will complete a 100-mile race. Since February of 2018, when I decided to take control of my life, my health, and my relationships to a new level, I had no idea that running would take my life in such a positive direction.

Thank you for reading. I hope to inspire others who claim that "they can't be a runner" to re-think that narrative what is possible for them and to just go for it. To start small, and not get overwhelmed when you have a bad day. We are all going to have bad training runs, bad attitudes when the weather sucks, and days when the weather is perfect, yet still don't have a good run. That's life. Setbacks are natural, it's how we respond to those natural setbacks and slingshot ourselves to heights we never thought possible.

I can't wait for May.

Louis Hylands

My name is Louis Hylands and I am 38.

I have been running now for five years, but only seriously for 18 months. My journey started in Kenya with a half marathon around Lakipia Airbase.

My furthest distance to date is 66 miles over two days during the Pilgrims Path and single day distance is 43.8 miles for the Country to Capital. I am looking to push out to 100 miles next year though and I also have an entry into the Fire + Ice Ultra in Iceland for 2020 which is multi-day over 250 kilometres.

The Country to Capital took place on the 12th of January 2019 and involved running from Wendover to Little Venice; I was drawn to it primarily for where it finished. My prep for the event was hampered by an Iliotibial Band Syndrome (ITB) problem that flared up during a marathon I ran in December; this also caused me some issues during the race itself, but I was able to dig deep and finish. Reaching the finish line was an amazing experience because at times I did not think I would make it. I was very fortunate to group up with three people a couple of miles from the finish, without their encouragement the last part would have been far more difficult. I was also very glad for the support of my good friend Tom, who came up to crew for me.

I run six times a week, I don't follow any real training plan I just go as little or as far as I feel like going on that day. I'd say I average around 40 miles a week though.

I just enjoy being outside, it's a great way to be around nature and also run off any stress from the day's work. Living by the sea, I am fortunate enough to have some beautiful views when I run. I'm also fairly close to Butser Hill, which has some amazing trails and scenery around it. These are my favourite runs as I enjoy the challenge of the hills and the views.

Running has been instrumental in helping my mental health. I have battled alcoholism, depression and an eating disorder when younger; there were times when I was at my lowest that I felt like giving up. This probably sounds selfish and I guess to some people it probably is, but when you're at your lowest you don't want to feel happy, you just don't want to feel at all. Anything is better than the constant sadness and darkness that takes over. Running has enabled me to feel like I am taking some control back; it allows me to feel free and at one with nature. Had I not taken up running I know I would have regressed back to alcoholism, I also would have struggled to cope with the loss of my brother and the ending of a long-term relationship. I've been dry nearly three years now and running has been key in that. I boxed for a while too but running has always been my passion. I've been lucky enough to strike up some strong friendships through my journey and gotten to know people closely who've also battled; without running I may not have had that opportunity. It's also given me an opportunity to become an ambassador for a mental health non-profit and raise money for Mind.

I love running because I can push myself as hard as I need to, I can enjoy it alone or with friends. It's taken me to places I may not have visited and allowed me to see some beautiful places. It's one of the few sporting endeavours I took up when I was ill that I stuck to, in fact it is the only one I stuck to!

The simplicity of it also helps, just put one foot in front of the other until you cross the finish line. When the legs say stop, will them to move forward with strength of mind.

What does running teach me about life? Well, it's like the journey we travel through life and also when the run is difficult, it's like going through tough times. If you keep going, eventually there is a finish line and it feels good to get there. It's an equaliser too; all people of all colours, creeds and beliefs can come together to share in the joy of running and movement. There are no barriers, we are just people that have come together to enjoy something we love and share the feeling of achievement. If we could also see life like that, the world would be a far happier place, I think.

I have a few running goals, the first being to finish the Fire + Ice in 2020, this is the trip of a lifetime and will be my biggest running challenge to date, I'll be doing it to raise money for good causes, which is an added bonus. Secondly in 2020, I'd like to go back and finish the Serpent Trail 100km, I took a DNF here last year as I struggled with the heat and the anti-depressant medication I was on. There is also a 100-miler in my sights, the Robin Hood and again this is a 2020 milestone. Longer term, Ultra Trails du Mont Blanc (UTMB), Squamish 50/50 and Cuyamaca 100km gives me a bit of an excuse to take a trip to the USA!

As I said earlier, I am 38, I'm also currently serving in HM Armed Forces and will be making history this year when I attempt the Royal Naval Physical Trainers Course as a Qualifier from the Army. I am the first person to be accepted from outside of the Royal Navy and Royal Marines. This is something I am very proud of. I've been written off a lot in the past and feel grateful to the Physical Training Branch for giving me the opportunity and also those who have guided me and helped shape me into the man I am now. It is my ambition to gain a BSc and a Masters in performance psychology in the following years; these are all things I would have never thought possible if I hadn't been able to straighten my life out. I feel thankful to have found running when I did.

In the past year I've also competed in the Hurtwood 50km (which was as tough as the name sounds!) and the 54321 50km in Salisbury – if you are someone wanting to start on an ultra journey the 54321 is a great place to begin.

Liz McCarthy

1) When you first started running

I started running as my commute to work after I had my first child in 2001. Having a baby had left me feeling a loss of identity (I was always a mum, colleague, wife, housekeeper, friend, etc.) so I carved out the very start of each day – while everyone else was still fast asleep – and started running in the morning darkness, relishing being alone with myself for the five-mile distance from home to office.

Five miles started off taking me about an hour but I slowly got the hang of it and sped up a little. I'm still a 9-10 minute miler but I like to stretch my selfish running time to about 15 miles a day. "I would compete against my own time and challenge myself to go farther than I believed I could," Liz remembers. "And I thought, 'maybe I'm ready to try a real race.'"

2) What is the furthest distance you have run; how long did it take and when? Please include the name and location of the race. Your preparation, how the race went and how you felt afterwards

The furthest I have run in one stint is 100km (62 miles) – I have managed this twice. My first was a London to Brighton ultra-marathon with Action Challenge. It was tough going but with each pitstop the realisation that I could actually do this grew and on finishing (after 15 hours) I felt incredibly elated!

The event was so well organised and supported that I booked the Bath to Cheltenham 100km with them the year after that first one. That was an intense event as the hills were constant and very steep. Running down steep inclines is a killer on the knees! I was the 27th lady to finish the event which took 15.5 hours!

A couple of years after that I booked with the same company to do the 106km (65 miles) circuit around the entire Isle of Wight. I liked the idea of running around an entire island. It was a blazing hot 28-degree day and my body gave up at 41 miles unfortunately because they forgot to supply electrolytes. I consider this unfinished business and will try it again next year!

3) How often you run

I run six mornings a week – only resting one morning because I know I have to for the sake of my joints, muscles and bones. I'd happily run more if my body would let me without getting injured.

4) What you enjoy about running

I love the peace and quiet with time in my head. I love being outside in all weathers, in touch with the real world (as opposed to the office) choosing whether to run in the streets, parks or from landmark to landmark. I love the selfish time in my own thoughts with space for my mind to freewheel and process whatever comes to mind.

5) How running helps your mental health

Running is essential for my mental health as it is the only time each day when I can think freely. It feels a bit like meditation – I just move, breathe and set my mind free. Of course, achieving very long runs has been good for my self-esteem (which is never great) as I know I have done something not many others have done, but that high is short-lived and it's the daily time with myself that is most healing.

6) Why you enjoy running

As above and because I can eat as much chocolate as I like and still stay healthy and slim.

7) What running teaches you about life

Running teaches me that if you put your mind into achieving something, it can be done. This seems to need to be re-learnt very frequently, however. Running has also taught me to be ok with my own thoughts.

8) Any future running goals?

That 106km around the Isle of Wight!

To raise more money to Macmillan Cancer Support – I enjoy having a platform for sharing why this charity is so important.

9) Anything you want to include about your job, family, where you live, where you are from and future life situation and goals?

It should be mentioned that running frequently brings injury. I have so far managed to tear a tendon in my ankle, fracture my pubic bone from top to bottom and my lower back is very twinge-prone because I run with a backpack on.

Please see below about my journey with dealing with cancer in others and with my own tumour. Running gave me space to process the traumatic journey for myself and family members.

Samantha Mills

I can remember coming to an absolute stop about 4 miles away from the A100 finish, a 100-mile race in Oxfordshire, run by Centurion. I turned to my pacer and my good friend and screamed at him that I was angry. I hadn't had an epiphany. I hadn't cried. I hadn't learnt anything on this journey and I had been robbed.

The clock was ticking and I had trained for months to be able to complete the race with a time that had '24' in it. It had been more of a struggle than I initially thought. With four kids, one who still breastfeeds, and a full-time job working with children in care, I questioned whether or not I would toe the line at all.

At that moment, when I stopped, I wanted an answer to something. To the why or the hows, or something, to prove the weirdly spiritual contact that I usually had with trail running that was now missing; it was nowhere to be found. I looked at my pacer and tried to squeeze out a tear. Nothing. In true form my pacer grabbed me mid-rant, turned me towards the end and said matter of factly: "You are heading to beat my first 100-miler time. Get f@*king on with it."

I looked at him and realised that he was right. It was time to get the job done. I ran the last 4 miles and hit the end with a finish time of 24 hours and 29 minutes. I was elated. I wasn't tired. I felt I had more to give and I had done it. Mum of four.

Former child in care. I had done it. Still no tears.

I still look back at that race in awe. It was the easiest hardest thing I had ever done and yet, for the first time ever, it made me question why I run. Over the last two years, since the race, I have battled and won against the Lavaredo Ultra Trail (LUT) with an injury that left me unable to run for the four weeks leading up to the race. A race that I had started and not completed twice before. The first time in 2011, I had blagged the race entry, embellishing my experience, certain that if I was able to run a marathon I would be able to run 90 km over 5,400m of ascent. I got in. It was my first ultra. I showed up in road shoes, having never run with a hydration pack, with no clue how to navigate, and not enough hills in my legs. I didn't finish.

From that moment on I vowed that I would return to finish what I had started. Unfortunately for me, that year the course record was smashed, so the North Face decided to increase both distance and elevation. It didn't deter me, but I realised that I would have to take mountain running and trail ultras a bit more seriously if I wanted to stand a chance.

In 2016 I tried again and failed. Fourteen months after having my fourth child, Genevieve and I boarded a flight to Munich then drove the four hours to Cortina to try again. I had trained hard, put in more hills, travelled miles with the buggy. It was right that she was there too.

I managed a good start, but it wasn't enough and by the halfway point I had less than 30 minutes for cut-offs and Genevieve was waiting for a feed. I knew that was the end of my second attempt. Genevieve came first; as I fed her watching and cheering as people went through Cimabanche, I once again vowed to try again.

That night, awake with ultra-lag having run through the night before, as I watched the head torches wind their way through the woods into Cortina from my window, I swore that my third attempt would be my last and that I wouldn't let the race beat me.

Running has taught me that sometimes what you know isn't enough and that when you need support it is best to ask professionals, so with my first 100 looming I took on a coach, Sarah Sawyer, and have yet to look back.

My entire mentality towards running has changed since. Not only did I realise that I had never trained enough hills for LUT, but that I was also overtraining and not training smart. It's been a steep curve, but I have finally come to realise that it is about the journey and that the journey is infinitely better if you are prepared.

Needless to say that my third attempt at LUT I completed. I had 100,000ft of ascent in my trained legs and though I was injured I made it. It wasn't pretty, but crossing the line after running through two nights and a series of hallucinations that I will never forget – Anne Frank in the trees; cheering rocks; a near-death experience and almost a paracetamol overdose – was the best feeling I have ever had.

I fought hard for that gilet. It is the only bib number I have ever framed. It is there to remind me that I can do whatever I put my mind to. That failure is just a learning process. But also to remind me that I couldn't do it alone, that my family are the most important thing in the world to me and that without my husband, who is my rock, and a family motto of 'never give up, never give in', none of it would be possible.

I have trained through rain, snow, sleet, heat and fog. I run up to 50 miles a week. I run with a buggy, I run at 3am to get the long ones in and not interrupt the finite balance between hobby and selfishness.

I run to feel. I run to forget and I run to remember, but mostly I run because I enjoy it. I enjoy the constant and consistent breath, heartbeat and footfall. I run to turn my mind off and be in the moment.

I learn from every run, but I learn most from the days when I don't want to. The days when it is too early, too dark, too rainy. The early mornings when I have been awake all night with one of the kids. Those days when I get out anyway help me to understand that whatever it is that makes me, me, is intrinsically linked to movement. It makes me realise that I am not a product of my past. That I am resilience, I am whatever I make of myself, and I am a runner.

Jude Hancock

My journey to ultra-marathon running started in 2016 when I decided I wanted to do a triathlon before I turned 40 years old. The problem was I couldn't run (at all). I'd been working crazy hours to make ends meet, and was feeling pretty fat and unfit (and I was). Luckily at the time I was thinking about this goal my local running club was advertising: a 10-week sofa-to-5km course, so I signed up. Two months after the sofa to 5km I did the triathlon which went well. I joined the running club as there was so much support from people who really could run. I spoke to people in the club who ran ultra-marathons, but in 2016 it wasn't something I wanted to do.

Looking back, 2016 was an interesting year. I didn't really get the 'buzz' from running that everyone spoke about until that summer when I joined the club on a trail run. It was hard work heading up the hills on uneven ground, but once up there the views were worth it. Over the next year I avoided tarmac and got on the trails. I also read Richard Askwiths' *Running Free* which was a eureka moment for me. I stopped worrying about not getting faster, and just went out enjoying free time plodding along in the countryside. It was (and still is) a way to think through the day that's been or the day ahead (even a bit of both if I get a lunchtime run in).

Towards the end of 2017 I decided that I wanted to do an ultra-marathon, just to see if I could do the distance. So instead of doing the sensible thing and signing up for a 50km event, I signed up for Race to the Stones (RTTS), 100km non-stop for July 2018. The finish for this event is a 30-minute drive from home, so my logic was 'well I can train on the route'. As this was going to be my first ultra, I downloaded the RTTS 20-week training plan and doubled it making it into a 40-week plan. During those 40 weeks I entered a few events that were on similar terrain (e.g. the Ridgeway 40) and gradually increased my mileage. A fellow club member also decided to sign up for the event (her first ultra, too). We trained together when we could and asked the experienced ultra-runners in the club about their experiences and top tips. Over a nine-month period it was a huge learning curve, how to map-read, how to snack while still moving forward, how to layer up in order to cope with the ever-changing Great British weather, and how to stop your water bladder from sloshing around (you turn it upside down and suck the air out). The unexpected snow in March 2018 didn't stop training; it just meant we got to practice the walking bit. It's one of the things I found weirdly quite challenging, for many of us, ultras are about running the downhills, walking up the hills to conserve energy, and a run/walk ratio on the flat. When you do your sofa-to-5km course it's all about running continually, but a novice ultra-runner needs to learn it's not all about continuous running.

So, did I complete RTTS? Yes. Did my training partner? No. My training partner had an accident during the event and withdrew at 13 miles. So mentally that was tough for me. Although I'd trained a lot on my own it was something we were going to achieve together, so heading off for 49 miles alone (well, not really, there were hundreds of other people doing the event) I had to get myself mentally in another frame of mind. I knew I had to cross that finish line for us both, and complete my own personal challenge. I'd aimed to complete RTTS in 14-16 hours, and finished in 18 and a half hours. The first 50km (despite the drama) I was on track and did this in 8 hours 5 minutes, but the second 50km were going fine until the last check-point (88km) when my legs decided they would carry me forward but only walking. So, the last 12km took two hours!

The day after the event, after only a few hours' sleep, I gingerly got out of bed and was pleasantly surprised I could walk fine, getting down the stairs wasn't the challenge I'd been expecting either. So, despite the event being different to what I'd envisaged, I was proud of what I'd achieved and knew from how I felt I'd done enough preparation. The week after RTTS I did a lot of walking and yoga, six days after I ran at my local parkrun and again was pleased that I was running my normal pace for that course.

Running has reiterated what I already know from my professional life, you need goals, but you need a realistic plan of how you are going to achieve these, and most importantly you need to stick to this plan as much as life will allow you. There will be times when you have to adapt your plan due to illness, work and family commitments, but a challenging day at work is not a reason to skip training. I would argue that a run mentally helps to cope with that difficult day.

Mentally, running can also be challenging, there will be people who will make remarks (e.g. about your slow pace) but my advice to others is that it's about your own personal achievements, try not to let the negative comments and negative people impact you (inevitable though it will be at times, especially if it's after a challenging day you've just had!). If you're fortunate to have a running club locally go along and see if it's for you. Our club has a great mix of runners of all distances and speeds. I am now a Leader in Running Fitness for the club and enjoy taking people out for a social plod. I have ultra goals for the foreseeable future, but I also enjoy seeing other people reach theirs (ultra and non-ultra-running related).

James Wright

I used to run when I was a kid, but stopped not long after I got picked in the cross-country team and kept coming last. I started again when I was at university in west Wales, running on the beach mainly, but then I fell into the world of beer, sport on TV and other non-running types of student activities. I didn't start again properly until about 10 years ago when a friend asked if I would run with him to lose weight.

Between us we slowly stepped up our distances until we completed marathons together. During this time, I've had two children, got married, moved house countless times and continued to work in a job that doesn't thrill me anymore.

I never set out to run an ultra, but I never set out to run a marathon either, it was the 1% statistic that got me, I think, that so few had done what I was doing, that and the fact I knew deep down I wanted my two young boys to be proud of me, and I loved their faces when I crossed the line and got a hug.

So, it never seemed odd to me to run beyond a marathon, 26 miles had always felt good, I was always better at running long rather than sprinting. I've run three ultras now in the last two years, one as pair, two on my own. The first two were both similar distances, 34 miles-ish, one in Tiree, Scotland, one on the Bronte moors in Yorkshire near where I live. Then last year seemed to be the perfect time to progress and to go further, so I did the 100km Race to the Stones. I'm planning maybe three or four this year and hoping to go further again on one of them, at 80 miles.

I don't often run more than three times a week, unless I'm really into the depths of training for an event that scares me. If I am really training then I'll be out four or five times a week with some Pilates or spinning thrown in. But if I'm honest that volume grinds me, especially if I have to run at lunchtimes at work to get miles on my feet, running on the canal in Leeds for so many years now is almost a punishment.

What I really like are the long runs, off road, like all my ultras have been. On the hills and dales, I think that's what attracts me. I've birdwatched since I was a kid and all my family holidays as a child were to the wild places of the UK. I love the big sky and the shifting clouds, I can lose myself looking at butterflies along the hedges or watching rabbits in the fields.

I loved my first ultra, running with my friend. He was fitter than me, and better on hills, but we did really well, the only problem I found was after 26 miles I had a real brain block. I had never gone that far before, in training or in a race and I think I freaked out, the next 4 miles were hell, all uphill, I walked nearly all of them. I would have given up and pulled out if I was on my own, but then on the crest of the hill I could see where I was going and the fog of my brain lifted. I nailed the last 2-3 miles, running like I had the wind at my back. Amazing thing, the human brain.

My second ultra, Tiree, was beautiful, my first solo, it's an incredible place, one lap round the island, a good mix of terrain, beautifully organised. I've realised since that for 10 miles or so I was running with a friend of mine who I had bumped into, and I now realise why I didn't like my 100km Race to the Stones. It took me 90km to find someone to talk to, even though I had great support at the checkpoints, my charity met me at half-way, my family met me at three or four places on route as well, but it wasn't the same as chatting whilst I moved. And I think that's why when I look back, I just didn't get a buzz from that race like I have in others.

Running on new trails thrills me. I think I like to see where paths go and how they link together, I like the not knowing, and I like the knowing even more.

I get stressed by life and I'm a worrier by nature. Running doesn't stop this, and sometimes I can't tell if it makes me better or not, but my wife says it does.

I have a feeling that I want my kids to be proud of me running, because I don't want them to think of me in the same way as I thought of my dad for a few years, and whilst one part of me knows that's a bit daft and I should just play Lego with them and run around the garden, the other part of me wants them to think dad's a superhero.

I couldn't tell you what gets me round those long lonely miles of training on the fells on my own, Tailwind and marmite sandwiches perhaps, but I've noticed the training doesn't seem to be lonely, (unless it's on a canal towpath) which is in itself odd given how I felt at Race to the Stones. I rarely train with others, but have happily run 35 miles or so on my own and have a great time in my own company. The wildlife and the views do help though, it might be accidental mindfulness.

I'm planning two or three ultras this year, the Calderdale Way, the Dales Way and maybe something called the Yorkshire Trod. The Dales Way will be the furthest I've ever gone, at 80+ miles, but it's beautiful, and it's a summer race, so I'm hopeful for the weather. The other two are really chuffing hilly so I'll have to see how I get on with those, as I'm hoping to get in the Yorkshire Three Peaks race this year too.

I'm not sure what the future holds as I promised my wife I'd stop running long distances once my youngest son was able to run and hug me at the end of the London Marathon, so I'm still trying in the ballot. I might try to run 100 miles before that happens, not sure, I'll see how 80 feels first. But I don't think I'd go beyond that.

I have my eye on a couple of multi-day events, and I've seen a couple of runs abroad, both would be a new experience, and I'd like to run more in the high fells of the Lake District and the mountains of Scotland, but it's all a balance with family life

Maybe I'll get a bike when that's all done and try to build up to an Ironman, but I'm no good in the water, so I'd need to practice that. It's good to have a hobby and a goal though. If I didn't have a goal to aim for, I'd just sit and eat crisps all day and my trainers would never see the light of day.

Michael Creighton

We are all born curious, our minds new and open to every possibility of the world around us, our little feet carried us forward, fear unknown and unfettered by the troubles of this new life or what is to come. Some of us lose that curiosity, we wander through our life feeling happy, we go on holiday, start and end both friendships and relationships, get jobs, buy houses and generally feel fulfilled. I'm no different.

My earliest memory of running, like most, is as a child. I was raised in the outdoors, we lived close to the Lake District and my father worked in the forestry industry making me fortunate that I was able to explore the quiet and wild woodlands and forest of the UK, my summer holidays spent playing, exploring and running around these massive and maze-like alien worlds. I was never really a runner though, I hated sports at school, being 15st made any physical activity a task to be hated rather than enjoyed. The annual cross-country run would swing by every year forcing the children of the year out onto the local fields and hills, more often than not it would rain heavily making the event that little bit worse.

I would wonder why people would choose to put themselves through what I felt was agony, watching them from the safety of the car as they ran, sweating, panting and red-faced towards and from nothing. I dabbled in mountain biking through my teens, more to lose the weight that made me sometimes unhappy with how I looked. I slimmed down and joined a gym, running the never-go-anywhere treadmill cramped in a warm, sweaty room with others struggling to make themselves into something else.

I lost the drive to exercise as I left for university, three years of mental health nursing followed, parties, drunken nights and fun-filled times, before I gained a role working in an acute psychiatric ward. I settled down with my wonderful partner and again gained weight which just snuck up on me like an artery-clogging ninja.

We rescued a small border collie puppy, she had an energy I had not seen before and exercise for me was back on the cards, I became a reluctant runner, at first feeling slightly embarrassed that I struggled to run even a mile, I became that red-faced sweaty person I would laugh at as a child, but unlike those days I grew fitter, I grew to love the trails and the woodlands that I found locally, importantly I found that it was an escape and my mind would calm and focus on nothing but being out.

It's unusual that you hear much from people like me (mental health nurses). We tend not to talk about everything that we see and hear each day. We see people at their worst, those that wish to take their own lives, those that have suffered unimaginable trauma and grief. We hear what you say and take that with us, we live your experience through you and try to help your mind and spirit.

We also remember those that didn't make it and live with the pain. We often find maladaptive coping mechanisms ourselves to carry on.

Running for me has become my escape, my switch off from the work I do and the ever-busy world we now live in. I can zone out, feel the wind and the rain, stand still and listen to the wildlife and sometimes silence around me. I would never have imagined that in the early days of my struggles that I would ever dream of running as I do now. My first trail event involved 13 hilly miles around the Long Mynd in Shropshire, I had entered the marathon but after the first 13 miles I was done, my legs burned and I struggled to breathe. A medal was given and a new sense of achievement gained.

I began running every other day, settling into a consistent routine of miles. I failed to follow any form of training plan, I'm just not that disciplined and I chose to listen to my body running different distances and stopping when I ached too much or increasing as I saw fit. Most people increase their miles slowly, a half marathon, a marathon, an ultra. I've always struggled to hold back, wanting to push faster, my mind making me feel more awesome than my body would allow. My first marathon was run at the same time I ran my first ultra event, the Black Country Ultra, 32 miles of stunning industrial canals around the West Midlands. I celebrated with a chap also running his first marathon and ultra; we trudged home together we thanked each other for the support and on we went, medal and T-shirt in hand. I've run only a few more organised ultra events, my furthest being 40 miles, through the night and alone. Escape from Meriden is one of the most epic ultras I've tried so far, self-supported, the route totally up to the escapees. I ran from Meriden in Coventry and ended my run with shin splints and sore feet at Castle Donnington. I was some 5 miles from my end point and ready to quit, but my wonderful partner came to my aid, gave me a kick up the arse and on I went – with her constant encouragement I finished the longest run I had ever run. I spent weeks recovering from that one but felt insanely happy that I had managed such a feat.

I've learned a lot from my running, I've learned that I am capable of much more than I thought I ever was. I always remind myself of what my parents were told when I was born, in February 1983. The nurses discovered that I was born with only my thumb on my right hand, the doctor's predicted that I would never be able to achieve much in my life due to this (I know, right!!). I am now able to laugh at this, their short-sightedness and the stupidity of these trained professionals who we entrust our lives to, judging me before I even had a chance, just out of the womb. But now I stand proud of what I have gained, my ability to run, my compassion and fortitude to challenge preconceptions of a world that at the time (remember it was only in the 1980's) struggled to know what inclusion meant.

This attitude has propelled me forward in my life, to challenge what I can do, to do it for myself and no-one else. 2019 sees the culmination of this attitude, I have challenged myself to run every UK National Park, unsupported and carrying everything that I will need to eat, sleep and recover with.

There are 15 parks in total spread across the UK, each park offers its own challenges and problems, some I have walked in before, some I have never trodden in, some are full of people, some are free from people and I will be many miles from any human touch.

In a way I am nervous but also enthralled by what is to come, having started and run my first park in January 2019, I have learnt that project will grow into something more than I first imagined. I met some unimaginably wonderful and kind people, offering their time to let me tell them my story of what I am doing, offer food and drink, to offer a stranger money for the charities that I am supporting, these are the moments that I will take with me, the honest and open kindness from people I have yet to meet. Strangers are only strangers until we say "hello".

Running has taught me a lot over the years. I remember sitting in the middle of Kinder Scout, having spent the night wild camping, and running back to my car. After some 50 miles of running, I lost a shoe in a bog. I sat, stared into the black hole and laughed. I laughed at the daftness, the silly mistake of not tightening my laces properly, but I wasn't scared or worried. I was miles from anyone, it was 6am on a wet and misty morning and no-one knew I was there. I gathered myself together and ran the last 4 miles home with just one trainer on, I knew from this point that there was little that could phase me if I just stopped and took stock of what was happening, slow my mind, my worries. I'm generally a solo runner, spending my runs in the wild moorlands of the UK, I tend to favour what to some may be lonely and desolate places, but I find a source of beauty therein, a canvas clean of distraction.

With each run I take, I gather a sense of fulfilment and achievement, any distance run is something we should thank ourselves for, we ran it our way, it was our race and we won for us.